LONDON, NEW YORK,
MELBOURNE, MUNICH, AND DELHI

Written and edited by Samone Bos, Phil Hunt, Andrea Mills
Art Editors Joanne Little, Johnny Pau, Owen Peyton Jones, Stefan Podhorodecki, Samantha Richiardi, Jacqui Swan, Rebecca Wright

Senior Editors Julie Ferris, Sarah Larter
Senior Art Editor Smiljka Surla

Managing Editors Lin Esposito, Camilla Hallinan
Managing Art Editor Diane Thistlethwaite
Design Development Manager Sophia M Tampakopoulos Turner
Publishing Managers Caroline Buckingham, Andrew Macintyre
Category Publisher Laura Buller

Picture Researchers Marian Pullen, Frances Vargo
Production Controller Erica Rosen
DTP Designer Andy Hilliard
Jacket Designer Neal Cobourne
Jacket Editor Mariza O'Keeffe

Consultants Ian Graham, Henry Hope-Frost, Brian Lavery, Chris Sidwells, Hugo Wilson, Christian Wolmar
Additional text by Clare Hibbert

First American Edition, 2006

Published in the United States by
DK Publishing, Inc.
375 Hudson Street
New York, New York 10014

Copyright © 2006 Dorling Kindersley Limited

06 07 08 09 10 10 9 8 7 6 5 4 3 2 1

A catalog record for this book
is available from the Library of Congress

ISBN-13: 978-0-7566-2224-4
ISBN-10: 0-7566-2224-7

Color reproduction by Colourscan, Singapore
Printed and bound by Hung Hing, China
**Discover more at
www.dk.com**

Ellington Middle School
Library Media Center

GO!

Contents

Introduction

Our lives are a series of journeys. They can be short walks or long-haul flights, taxi rides or a vacation cruise—as technology and innovation transform transportation by air, land, and water, never before have we gone so far so fast.

GO! takes us on a trailblazing visual journey. It is an eye-popping exploration of the world of travel, from the ordinary to the extraordinary. Without taking a step, we will shoot over land on a bullet train, zip across the skies in a giant Airbus, sail the seas in a sleek superyacht, and leap from a plane with just a parachute. In three thematic chapters devoted to water, land, and air, *GO!* lifts the lid on the ways that people travel from A to B. We visit transport hubs all around the world and get firsthand accounts from passengers and workers. We peel back the roof of a jumbo jet, and pull apart all types of transportation, from a classic car to a racing sailboat. Along the way, we witness hair-raising motocross stunts, glimpse a speeding rocket-powered car, and peer into airline air-sickness bags. Our fascinating journey spans all five continents, going as far back as the first human footprint and as far forward as space tourism. Just where will we go next?

Water

10

Timeline

EARLY RAFT BOAT

First record of rafts
Migrants traveling from Southeast Asia reach Australia on rafts made of logs and reeds. This is the first record of rafts being used, and the migrants are Australia's first inhabitants.

GREEK VASE ENGRAVING

Greek warships
Galleys—large, shallow ships with sails and oars—are used as warships by the Greeks. They customize the design by adding a battering ram to smash enemy vessels.

BOW OF LONGBOAT

Viking longboats
The sight of distinctive Scandinavian longboats fills the people of northern Europe with fear. The Vikings launch raids from Scandinavia every summer in these vessels. Longboats carry armed warriors and their horses, and move easily in open sea and shallow rivers.

DISCOVERY OF NEW FOODS

Global exploration
Explorers use sailing ships to discover new lands. When Christopher Columbus leads an expedition across the Atlantic, he also finds new produce such as potatoes and tomatoes.

BRITISH 70-GUN TWO DECKER

Men-of-war
Sailing ships become fast and effective floating fortresses. European navies compete with each other by building heavily armed fighting ships called "men-of-war."

▲ c. 5000 BCE c. 3100 BCE ▼ ▲ c. 1000 BCE c. 1 CE ▼ ▲ 800 CE 1200 ▼ ▲ 1492 1600 ▼ ▲ 1650 1661 ▼

Sail technology
Ancient Egyptians build sailboats for fishing and transporting goods. They are the first people to use sails. This depiction of a sail painted on a vase is the first recorded use of a sail. The rectangular sails speed up travel along the slow-moving Nile River, but oars are still used to steer the boats.

VASE PAINTING OF EGYPTIAN SAIL BOAT

ROMAN COIN SHOWING GALLEY

Warring galleys
The Romans reinforce the sterns of the basic galley design for greater defense in sea battles. The galley is now the fastest vessel at sea. Galleys are used in war in ancient Persia, Greece, and Rome right up until the 16th century.

Chinese junks
The South China Sea suffers typhoons, so the Chinese junk is designed with a very strong, rigid hull. Junk is Malayan for "boat."

MODEL OF CHINESE JUNK

MODEL GALLEON

Racing galleon
English slave-trader John Hawkins improves the basic Spanish galleon design. Known as the "race-built" galleon, the new vessel is lower in the water and much faster.

PAINTING OF FIRST YACHT RACE

Yacht race
The first recorded yacht race takes place along the Thames River in London, England. Two royal ships take part in the race—King Charles II's *Catherine* and the Duke of York's *Anna*. Following this grand occasion, yachting regattas grow in popularity.

STATUE OF CAPTAIN COOK

Voyage of discovery
On board his ship *Endeavour*, English explorer Captain James Cook sails more than 29,800 miles (48,000 km) on a three-year voyage of exploration, during which he charts New Zealand.

PAINTING OF CLERMONT

Introduction of steamboats
US engineer Robert Fulton invents the first steamboat. Called *Clermont*, the vessel successfully travels from New York City to Albany, New York State. The vessel is the first ever to be fitted with paddle wheels instead of sails.

PROPELLER FROM THE MAURETANIA

Propellers
The propeller is invented to replace paddles. It is more efficient and able to work better in choppy seas. Due to the propeller's position on a ship, it is less likely to be damaged in a collision with another vessel.

CROSS-SECTION OF A BATTLESHIP

Battleship development
Sea warfare is revolutionized by the development of battleships. These enormous vessels combine armor plating, steam propulsion, and guns. The gun turret is specially designed to fire shells over huge distances.

MAERSK SEALAND CONTAINER SHIP

Transatlantic containers
Despite the huge increase in air travel, 95 percent of goods are still transported by sea. The American SeaLand line begins containerized shipping between the US and Europe. Identical boxes are piled up on board so the ship can carry a greater load.

1768 1790 1807 1848 1850 1898 c. 1900 c. 1960 1966 2004

RESCUE LIFEBELT

Origins of the lifeboat
The first vessel specifically built to function as a lifeboat is constructed by Englishman Henry Greathead. Called *The Original*, it is launched on the Tyne River in England in 1790. The lifeboat makes its first rescue during the same year.

PANNING FOR GOLD

Gold rush!
When gold is discovered in California, prospectors travel from the East Coast and around the tip of South America to reach California in the west. Fast clipper ships, with their multiple masts and sails, transport the fortune hunters.

JOHN PHILIP HOLLAND

Prototype submarine
John Philip Holland devises a submarine prototype. His designs prove a success and are adopted by the navies of Britain, Japan, Russia, Germany, and Sweden. He is hailed as "the father of the modern submarine."

MODEL OF MOTORIZED YACHT

Pleasurecraft
Sailing the seas becomes a leisure pursuit for many people and, to cope with the demand, varied types of pleasureboats and yachts are mass-produced. Racing yachts are constructed for use in competitions, and surfing takes off in the USA.

QUEEN MARY 2

Super ships
Ships increase in size, scale, and luxury as tourists enjoy around-the-world cruises with more facilities and ports of call. The largest liner in the world is the *Queen Mary 2*.

Ocean transporters

For thousands of years, boats and ships have transported people and goods all around the world. Their cargoes vary from fruit and fish to jeans and shoes; some may carry cars or aircraft parts, and others take passengers. For people living on remote islands, boats are often the only transport link with the outside world. Whether powered by oar, sail, steam, or diesel engine, these ocean transporters are vital to people's lives and livelihoods.

Junk

The Chinese perfected the junk design about 1,000 years ago. It has multiple masts, accordion sails, and a hull of watertight compartments. Merchant junks carried ceramics and silks to India, Arabia, and East Africa. Junks also engaged in sea battles and voyages of discovery, but now they are mostly used as family homes.

Sea barge

Designed for extremely heavy cargoes, a sea barge has the same capacity as 38 loaded river barges. Typical cargoes are dry bulk, such as coal or grain, and liquids, such as water or petrol. Military barges carry tanks or landing craft.

Dhow

Arab traders have used dhows to transport fruit, fish, and lumber around the Indian Ocean for more than 2,000 years. Traditionally, the lateen (triangular) sails were made from palm leaves and the hull planks were stitched together with cord.

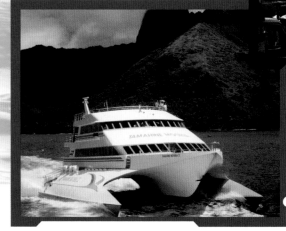

Hydrofoil

Built for speed and stability, a hydrofoil has a pair of wings or foils under the hull. As it accelerates, its hull lifts out of the water until only the foils are submerged. Hydrofoils have been used as passenger and car ferries since the 1950s.

Merchant ships

A merchant ship carries cargo from port to port. Smaller ships often service hub ports, where their cargoes are transferred to large container ships. They transport food, books, clothes, and electrical goods.

Naval ships

A variety of military ships are used for a range of missions. Some transport troops or essential supplies, while others patrol coastlines or drop touch-sensitive bombs called mines. Destroyers are among the most heavily armed warships in use today.

Outrigger canoe

Similar to stabilizers on a bicycle, outriggers are long floats that fix to each side of a boat and make it less likely to capsize. Outrigger canoes carried the first people to Polynesia from Southeast Asia about 5,000 years ago. Pacific islanders still use them for sea fishing.

Lepa

The Bajau people of Southeast Asia traditionally lived on wooden boats called lepa. They travelled from coast to coast, fishing and trading. Most Bajau have settled ashore now, but they continue to fish in their lepa. Many also take part in the annual lepa regatta at Semporna, Malaysia.

Basket boat

In Vietnam, fishermen paddle small basket boats. The boats are woven from thin strips of bamboo and have a waterproof, varnish coating. As well as being used for fishing, basket boats taxi tourists around the islands.

Superstitious sailors

In the face of uncontrollable weather and seas, it is no surprise that the sailing profession is so superstitious. The eyes seen painted on some Mediterranean boats are meant to deter the much-feared "evil eye," a superstition first referred to in texts dating back to 3000 BCE. According to folklore, one glance from a person who unknowingly has an evil eye can bring bad luck, disease, and death. Sailors also believe tattoos, black cats, rainbows, and horseshoes are lucky on board, while green boats, red hair, black traveling bags, and sailing on a Friday bring bad luck.

All in the name

Boat owners give a lot of thought to naming their vessels—a tradition started by the Ancient Egyptians thousands of years ago. Although no laws exist requiring boats to be named, almost all of them are. The most popular names include *Serenity*, *Sea Spirit*, and *Escapade*. It is also common for boat owners to name their vessels afer female family members. Renaming the boat at a later date is considered very unlucky and best avoided. If renaming is essential, the old name must be erased from everything, including shipping charts and log books.

Worn allegiance

Pride in a vessel and being part of a crew is integral to naval life, and wearing a uniform is one way to show affiliation. Naval crews of different nations, as well as various classes of ships, adopt individual uniforms. A higher-ranking crew member's uniform can be identified by special features such as a double-breasted blazer, gold stripes, and peaked cap. Shoulder patches are worn to represent a variety of achievements.

Flying the flag

Whether displaying country of origin, class of ship, or an individual insignia, flags are a common sight on every type of vessel. Naval ships hoist up national flags on entering and leaving harbor, while submarines fly their battle flags from the conning tower before submerging. Smaller yachts and boats sometimes rig up brightly colored miniature flags for decoration and to indicate wind direction.

Writing on the wall

When sailors dock in some Mediterranean ports, such as Funchal Harbor in Madeira, they paint pictures of their boats on the huge sea walls surrounding the harbors, including personal elements such as the names and on-board decorations that distinguish the boats. According to superstition, all sailors entering these harbors must draw their boats or add their vessel names to the walls to make sure they return to their home ports safely.

Shipping identity

Sailors must depend on their vessels—sometimes for their lives—and this often forges a strong attachment. They personalize their boats by giving them names, protect them with lucky talismans, and adorn them with flags, carvings, and decorations. Every boat has something that gives it its own individual identity.

- Pirates still attack ships, especially in the South China Sea, the Straits of Malacca, and off the coast of Brazil.

- The busiest container ports are Singapore, Hong Kong in China, and Rotterdam in the Netherlands.

- Cargo is stored on board in standard-length containers of 20 ft (6 m) and 40 ft (12 m).

- The world's largest container ship is MSC *Pamela*, built by Samsung Heavy Industries in 2005. The vessel is 1,053 ft (321 m) long and 148 ft (45 m) wide. If the containers were lined up end to end, they would span 35 miles (56 km).

- There are more than 350 container ships currently carrying passengers around the world. This figure is larger than the number of cruise ships in operation.

- The fuel burned by container ships is called "bunker 380." It has the consistency of tar and must be kept heated at to stop it frm turning into a solid lump in the fuel tank.

- A container ship carrying 1,600 containers burns about 40 tons of fuel every day.

Container ship

Containerization has transformed cargo shipping, making it much easier and quicker to carry goods across the seas. Before the 1950s, loading and unloading ships was slow and laborious due to the different sizes and shapes of the cargo. Huge container ships now hold goods in standardized steel boxes that pile up perfectly like building blocks. Nicknamed "box boats," these ships transport at least 200 million containers every year. The largest ships can carry more than 4,000 containers in one trip. Today, about 90 percent of the world's dry cargo travels on board container ships.

- Meat and fish are carried in temperature-controlled containers, known as "reefer containers," which have a refrigerator unit attached to one end.

- The average speed of a container ship is 20 mph (32 km/h). During the course of 24 hours, a container ship will travel on average 500 miles (800 km).

- Rain and seawater is drained away through a "scupper"—a tiny hole located on the top deck of a container ship.

- Each container is anchored by "twist locks," which twist to lock the eight corners of the container to the container next to it.

- Container ships must be loaded with care as improperly stored cargo makes a vessel unstable, particularly in stormy seas.

- The Brazilian wandering spider is known as the "banana spider" because some have been found on container ships carrying bananas to the US.

- The best-selling novel Roots was written on a container ship. Author Alex Haley was inspired by the peace and solitude.

- Most container ships have a crew of 30 people. The accommodation area is located at the stern, above the engine room.

- In 2002, the Norwegian-registered Tricolor was carrying $45-million-worth of luxury cars when it sank after a collision.

- Every year about 10,000 containers fall from ships and land in the sea. Storms are usually the cause of this.

- In 1992, several containers on a ship bound for the US fell overboard. As a result, about 29,000 plastic bath toys were left floating in the sea!

- American Malcolm McLean invented the concept of shipping containers in the 1930s.

- The first container ships were converted tankers, adapted after World War II.

Ship shape

Today's high-tech shipbuilding is a far cry from the art of the ancient shipwright, who spent months seasoning lumber, nailing hull planks, and stitching sails. Steel and state-of-the-art plastics have replaced wood, computers now assist with the design, cutting is carried out by robots, and cranes heave enormous prefabricated sections of the vessels into place. The biggest modern shipyards are in Asia, where land and labor are inexpensive. This is also where ships go to be broken up.

Hull construction
In a fountain of sparks, a construction worker welds steel plates onto the bulkhead of HMS *Tyne*, a warship. Protective coveralls, gloves, and goggles are essential for this dangerous work. Welding has been commonplace since World War II. Before then, the steel plates were fastened together with metal rivets.

Working with wood

This Turkish shipwright is working on a rib of a traditional wooden fishing vessel called a *çektirme*. Until the 19th century, most ships were built from lumber using one of two methods of construction: the first was to create a wooden skeleton, then nail on the hull planks. The second involved making the hull shell first, adding an internal framework later.

Dry dock

Hundreds of people are involved in the building of a ship, including engineers, welders, plumbers, electricians, painters, and carpenters. Construction often takes place in a dry dock to give workers complete access to the vessel. Wooden supports called stocks hold the ship in place.

Shipyard site

One of the world's largest shipyards is Daewoo in South Korea. China, Japan, and South Korea lead the way in shipbuilding and have huge steel industries to supply the raw materials. Shipyards sprawl along the coastlines, employing tens of thousands of people. Some produce as many as 70 large vessels every year.

Ship launch

Whether large or small, new ships are named prior to launch. The crude oil carrier NS *Challenger* was named at a special ceremony in January 2005. If the ship is on land, it is towed down a ramp into the sea. More often, the ship is in dry dock. This fills with water and the vessel is launched.

Regular maintenance

After launch, a vessel must still return to dry dock at various times during its life. Ships are regularly checked, repaired, and modified to ensure they stay safe and seaworthy. Workers here are cleaning an anchor to minimize the buildup of rust.

End of the liner

Once a vessel is old and unseaworthy, it is broken up for scrap and recycling. Most ships are dismantled at Chittagong in Bangladesh or Alang in India. Steel plates, machinery, and even toilets are salvaged. Crews work with little more than their bare hands, so accidents are common.

Oil!

Without oil, many of the journeys we take would not be possible. Powering our cars, boats, and planes, this fossil fuel is integral to our lives. Oil forms from the remnants of minute animals and plants that died in the world's oceans millions of years ago. As a result, oil is often found in remote parts of the seabed and must make a long journey of its own in order to become all the varied and useful products we recognize today.

Huge oil tankers, known as crude carrier tankers, carry 62 percent of the crude oil found at sea to refineries around the world. About 3,500 tankers are currently used to transport oil.

Knock Nevis, the world's biggest oil tanker

Oil production platform in the North Sea

On offshore oil platforms, workers use huge drills to dig deep down into the seabed for oil. An undersea pipe connects the platform to a loading rig, which fills either a tanker or a pipe with oil.

An underwater pipeline in the North Sea

About 38 percent of the world's oil is carried by undersea pipelines. Although pipelines are invaluable once built, they are generally very costly and complicated to lay under the sea.

Oil refinery in Montreal, Canada

Oil is transported to a refinery, an industrial plant where the impurities in crude oil are removed. The purified substance is distilled and undergoes other separation and refinement processes before it is turned into a range of by-products.

The variety of by-products are taken by tanker for delivery around the world. The tankers are enormous, often more than 1,475 ft (450 m) long, 197 ft (60 m) wide, and 80 ft (25 m) deep. Due to their size, tankers are hard to steer and it can take 15 minutes to bring one to a halt. Some crews cycle around the decks to save time.

Anchored tanker preparing to make a delivery of oil by-products

A section of the Trans-Alaska pipeline system

If a destination is landlocked, has a short coastline, or the distance to travel is reduced by taking a land route, then pipelines are used to transport the oil by-products instead of tankers. The pipes are usually above ground. If the area is built up or protected by conservation legislation, the pipes are laid 3 ft (1 m) underground.

A series of pump stations lining the horizontal pipes keep the oil by-products moving quickly to their destination. Without the pumps the liquid and gas products inside would be unable to flow along the pipes.

In 2005, 1.9 billion tons of crude oil were shipped around the world. The scale of this demand comes from the diverse range of products derived from crude oil. Aside from fuel for transportation, the end-products of oil are all around us, in paraffin, plastics, synthetics, rubber, waxes, and lubricants. From insecticides to perfumes, asphalt to detergents, and crayons to tires, oil proves a versatile, invaluable resource.

Aviation fuel and petrol are two of the major uses of refined oil.

Tanker offloading oil products in California

Pipelines link up to docks and cities where the by-products can be deposited. Similarly, tankers dock and deposit their by-products at ports all over the world. A system called Worldscale now regulates tankers. This ensures tankers carry products worldwide, and not just to affluent countries. Tanker owners earn a fixed rate regardless of the length or difficulty of the trip. On arrival, products are stored in containers, and trains or trucks are used to distribute them.

Oil facts and figures

- One barrel of oil is the same as 42 gallons (159 liters), which is enough to fill the gas tanks of four standard cars.

- The US uses almost 22 million barrels of oil every single day.

- The world's largest oil field is in Saudi Arabia. It is 43 miles (70 km) long and 19 miles (30 km) wide.

- In 1877, the first oil tanker, the steam-powered *Zoroaster*, was built to transport kerosene in the Caspian Sea.

- One of the largest oil pipelines is the Trans-Alaska pipeline system. It is 807 miles (1,300 km) long, and crosses three mountain ranges as well as 800 rivers and streams.

- The oil drill bit has industrial diamonds on the cutting edges. Diamonds are hard enough to cut through rock.

- In 1989, the *Exxon Valdez* tanker ran aground in Alaska, spilling 11 million barrels of oil. The clean-up cost for the first year was $2 billion.

Linking oceans

The Panama Canal is an artificial waterway connecting the Atlantic and Pacific oceans in Central America. Although its construction was one of the most difficult engineering projects in history, the end result has transformed the world's shipping routes for the better. No longer do ships need to travel the lengthy and dangerous path around Cape Horn at the southern tip of South America; instead, they can cut straight through the narrow strip of Panama. More than 850,000 vessels have used the canal since its completion in 1914.

Canal path
The Panama Canal spans 51 miles (82 km). It cuts through the country of Panama, connecting the Pacific Ocean with the Caribbean Sea and on to the Atlantic Ocean.

Hard task
For a decade, more than 40,000 workers, mostly from the Caribbean, worked to build the canal. Thousands died during construction, largely due to landslides and outbreaks of malaria.

Wide berth
With a minimum depth of 39 ft (12 m) and a series of locks (sets of gates that lift and lower ships between canal sections of different heights), all but the biggest vessels can pass through the canal.

Challenging locks
During construction, the enormous canal locks were a real challenge to build. The three sets of locks each stand 1,000 ft (305 m) in height, 108 ft (33 m) in width, and weigh 700 tons.

Water features
As well as the locks, the route includes three artificial lakes, one of which is larger and acts as a reservoir, providing extra water storage for the canal.

Floating crane
It takes almost 10 hours for a vessel to pass through the canal, and about 40 will pass through every day. One is the Goliath crane, which is on hand to lift and transport the heavy lock gates if they need to go for repairs.

Cutting continents

Built to provide the fastest crossing from the Atlantic Ocean to the Indian Ocean, the Suez is one of the world's largest canals and connects the Mediterranean Sea to the Gulf of Suez. Completed in 1869, this huge achievement was a combined effort by French and British engineers. Today, the Suez carries 14 percent of world shipping.

Super size
Unlike the Panama, the simpler Suez has no locks so almost any size and type of ship can pass through, includng oil platforms.

Single file
Most of the Suez Canal has room for only one lane of traffic. However, passing bays are scattered along the route.

Suez from space
The Suez Canal is so large that it can be clearly seen from space. Here, the Great Bitter Lake is visible at the canal's center.

Canal path
The Suez is 118 miles (190 km) long, with a minimum width of 197 ft (60 m). Ships can travel from Europe to Asia without circumnavigating Africa.

Mediterranean Sea

Suez

Gulf of Suez

Ports of call

Chennai, India
During the 1600s, the English East India Company began to trade from the fishing village of Chennai, in southeastern India. The fishing industry is still thriving today, but Chennai's three artificial harbors also handle more than 35 million tons of international cargo a year.

Most of the world's major cities are served by a port with commercial facilities where ships and boats can dock. Ports often bustle with activity as boats arrive and depart, cranes unload container ships, and workers busy themselves in local warehouses. A network of transportation links, such as railroads, roads, and rivers carries goods inland. Similar to ports, harbors shelter boats from the sea. Natural harbors are enclosed by land; artificial ones have sea walls. Harbors with special moorings for yachts are marinas.

Hong Kong, China
With its huge, sheltered natural harbor, Hong Kong is one of the world's busiest container ports. Around 220,000 vessels dock here each year. As well as container ships, there are passenger ferries, cruise liners, and oil tankers. Every June, the port hosts the city's famous dragon boat races.

CONTAINER PORTS

These ports cover a large area as the enormous container ships need room to dock. The equipment used to pack the goods on board and send them on to their final destinations also requires a vast expanse of space. Hong Kong, Shanghai, and Singapore are among the world's busiest container ports.

Rotterdam, The Netherlands

Europe's busiest port is Rotterdam. It is built around the Nieuwe Maas, a river connecting the Rhine and the North Sea. Crude oil, iron ore, and coal make up almost half of Rotterdam's cargo, and there are five oil refineries in the industrial area around the port.

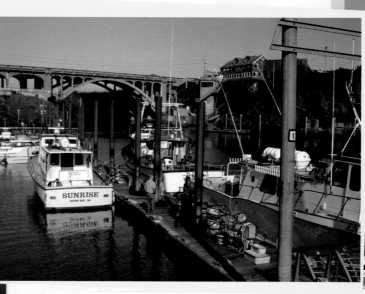

Depoe Bay, Oregon

The port of Depoe Bay on the Pacific coast is considered to be the world's smallest navigable harbor. The bay is landlocked, except for one small entrance through the tough basalt rocks that form the sides of the harbor. Fishing boats bring in salmon, halibut, and flounder, while charter vessels take people whale-watching.

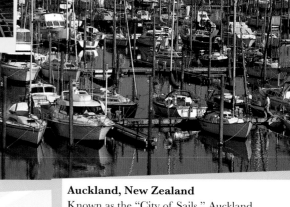

Auckland, New Zealand

Known as the "City of Sails," Auckland has hosted two America's Cup challenges. It has two harbors—Waitemata on the Pacific and Manukau on the Tasman Sea. Both are packed with yachts. In 2005, the first Auckland Harbour Festival took place, with tall ships races, yacht regattas, and fireworks.

FISHING PORTS

Every year, ships bring about 85 million tons of fish, shellfish, and mollusks into the world's fishing ports. Tuna is the main deep-sea catch. Most ports have a fish market, with Tokyo in Japan being one of the world's biggest. Many ports also have canning factories or processing plants.

RIVER PORTS

Not all ports are directly by the sea or ocean. They can also be situated on rivers, canals, or lakes. The port of Kampala, the capital of Uganda, lies on Lake Victoria. Some river ports, such as Rotterdam in the Netherlands, have links to the ocean along deep waterways.

MINIPORTS

Some harbors are so tiny that boats cannot even move around in them. The Italian island of Ginostra, for example, has a harbor that is just 10 ft (3 m) wide. Once inside, fishing boats have to be hauled on to a paved slope to make way for other incoming vessels.

PLEASURE PORTS

Ports around the Caribbean are very popular with yachtspeople because of the region's fine weather and good sailing conditions. There are 30 marinas in the Bahamas alone. Europe's most famous pleasure port is Monte Carlo, Monaco, on the Mediterranean coast.

The passengers

Every day, an eclectic mix of people use the Sydney Ferries: visitors from all over the world come to see the sights and enjoy the surrounding bays, commuters regularly catch boats to work, and locals find the vessels ideal for day trips.

Mac

Every morning, fisherman Mac returns with his catch for the market. "Fishing is really hard work. We do long hours and it gets very tiring," he explains.

Vincent

For 20 years, Parisian pastry chef Vincent has caught the first ferry at 5:40 a.m. "I grab a coffee, sit down, and admire the view."

Hilary

Hilary always chooses a window seat for her ferry commute to work. "I love the traditional, friendly ferries. They are the calmest way to travel."

John

With his passion for boats, John enjoys sightseeing tours by ferry. "The best time to go on a tour is at night when the city is all lit up."

Erin and Michael

On vacation from Melbourne, Erin and Michael enjoy the ferry tours. "The ferry is less stressful than car traffic," says Michael.

Nicole

Californian student Nicole is visiting Sydney. "The ferries are cheap, easy to ride, and ideal for visiting different, picturesque places."

Traveling on water

Commuters, locals, and tourists mingle at central Circular Quay where Sydney Ferries is based. From here, the ferries carry travelers to and from more than 40 wharves around the harbor at regular times throughout the day.

Harbour life

■ Established in 1788, Sydney Harbour was the first permanent European settlement in Australia.
■ In 2004, there were 4.3 million people living in Sydney and 2.6 million short-term visitors to the city from other countries.
■ Before the Sydney Harbour Bridge opened in 1932, 400 million passenger journeys were made on the ferries each year. Today, the ferries annually carry more than 14 million people around the city and the surrounding suburbs.
■ Circular Quay is the busiest transport hub in the whole of Sydney. As well as the ferry terminal, which has eight piers, it is also home to the city's main bus station and a train station linking the city center with the southern and eastern suburbs.
■ The thriving surfer's beach and café town of Manly is the most popular destination for ferry passengers.

Sydney Harbour ferries

Sydney is one of the most beautiful maritime citi[es in the] world. With its deep waters, coves, and inlets, it is [a] busiest port. The harbor throngs with cargo ships [carrying] millions of tons of imports and exports, luxury li[ners] docking for a stay in the city, pleasure cruisers soa[king in] the scenery, and fishermen landing catches from [the] Ocean. Every day, the harbor ferries carry comm[uters] to work and take tourists to see the iconic landma[rks.]

Syd[ney Harbour]
One of the largest n[atural harbours] in the world, Sy[dney Harbour] stretches 12 miles (19[km) and covers] an area of 34 sq m[iles.] The famous steel arch [bridge links] the north and so[uth shores.]

The workers

The running of Sydney Ferries Corporation is a real team effort. From the skippers steering the vessels to the deck hands and ticket sellers, the crew support each other in order to meet the demands of the busy ferry timetable.

Michael H

As part of Customer Services, Michael helps visiting tourists make best use of the ferries. "We suggest the most interesting routes."

John

Ferry engineer John maintains the boats. "I start the engines in the morning, check them throughout the day, and shut them down at night."

Gregory

Heading up a team of three, Greg is responsible for controlling ferry movements. "We have a million dollar view working here," he says.

Michael B

Passenger care and docking ferries are deck hand Michael's concerns. "The best thing about my job is getting paid to be at Sydney Harbour."

Nada

Nada sells the ferry tickets to customers at the harbor kiosk. "We do three 12-hour shifts in a row so I drink a lot of coffee!"

Kris

There are about 80 captains working on Sydney Ferries and Kris is one of them. As skipper, he steers and navigates the vessel. He explains, "I started here as a deck hand and that was over 30 years ago!"

Fleet of ferries

- ■ Sydney Ferries have cruised around Sydney Harbour for more than 135 years.
- ■ The fleet consists of 31 vessels divided into seven classes. Each class of ferry carries a different number of passengers.

- ■ The largest class of ferry is the distinctive green and yellow Freshwater. There are four of these and each carries up to 1,100 passengers.
- ■ The smallest class of ferry is called RiverCat.

There are seven in the fleet, each carrying 230 passengers.
- ■ The fleet of ferries operates approximately 110,000 trips each year and annually travels about 808,000 miles (1.3 million km).

- ■ The network stretches 23 miles (37 km), with central Sydney at its core. It includes the nearby suburb of Parramatta in the west, the seaside resort of Manly in the northeast, and the fishing village of Watson's Bay in the east.

Water rescue

The ocean is a dangerous place with strong currents, shifting seabeds, and unpredictable weather. Rescue services are trained to respond to any emergency call-out and include large lifeboats, small inflatable craft, helicopters, individual lifeguards, and even dogs. They must go to the assistance of a swimmer swept out to sea, a diver drifting in shark-infested waters, a fishing boat lashed by strong seas, or an oil tanker breaking up on rocks. In the Arctic Sea, ice-breaker vessels cut a path through the ice to help container ships get past. In warmer parts of the world, the crews of boats caught up in tropical storms may need assistance. All around the world, many people owe their lives to these brave rescue teams.

Rescue records

■ Englishmen William Wouldhave (1751–1821) and Lionel Lukin (1742–1834) both claimed to have invented the lifeboat.

■ The first lifeboat was tested on the Tyne River in England on January 29, 1790.

■ The longest time adrift at sea was 484 days. Oguri Jukichi from Japan was stuck at sea when his ship was damaged in a storm. From October 1813, he drifted off the Japanese coast until he was finally rescued by a US ship off California on March 24, 1815.

■ The longest journey in a lifeboat was completed when Sir Ernest Shackleton took a small lifeboat called *James Caird* from Elephant Island to South Georgia. The distance covered was 800 miles (1,287 km).

■ When the ocean liner *Titanic* hit an iceberg and sank in 1912, it had only 20 lifeboats on board, capable of carrying just 52 percent of the passengers.

■ The largest totally enclosed lifeboat, known as a TELB, is the Norwegian Norsafe. It can carry 90 people and the cover protects against fire and toxic gases.

Modern lifeboats

Lifeboats are designed to be self-righting, which means they roll back to be the right way up if they capsize. The boats rely on Global Positioning Systems (GPS) and radar for navigation. They carry fire extinguishers, life buoys, distress flares, and pumps to remove water from sinking ships. First-aid kits, breathing equipment, blankets, and food and water are kept on board to treat survivors. The captain radios to shore if the lifeboat needs to be met by an ambulance.

Inflatable assistance

Most inshore life rafts are rigid inflatables with room for five people. If many survivors need to be picked up at once, such as after a plane crash, large inflatable platforms are used. These can be dropped from the air or thrown from a lifeboat or life raft.

Helicopter rescue

Helicopters airlift people to safety from the sea or drop life-jackets to keep people afloat until a lifeboat arrives. They also bring search-and-rescue dogs to the scene that can detect people under water. This dog is being trained to swim out to a victim.

Solo savers

In Australia, beachside water rescues are performed by individual lifeguards. Each lifeguard has a rescue surfboard, which doubles up as a stretcher, a rescue tube to tow survivors back to shore, and a pair of flippers to help swim quickly to an emergency.

Underwater world

With more than two-thirds of the Earth's surface covered in ocean, it is no wonder that people are eager to explore it. Pioneering designs and developments in the form of apparatus, vehicles, and vessels are opening up our oceans as never before. From the sparkling surface to the darkest depths, people can now view marine creatures, salvage wrecks, study water life, and monitor oil platforms.

Sea level
0 ft
(0 m)

20 ft
(6 m)

65 ft
(20 m)

165 ft
(50 m)

675 ft
(200 m)

❶ **Glassbottom boat**
Boats with sections of glass below the waterline enable passengers to view the marine world without even getting wet. Issues such as safety and use of breathing apparatus do not matter as tourists sit back and enjoy the onboard comforts. These trips are popular in clear, warm waters where marine life flourishes and tourists are guaranteed sightings of underwater creatures and plants.

❷ **Snuba**
This is a hybrid form of snorkeling and scuba diving. Divers use standard scuba breathing apparatus, but the compressed air tanks are located on floating rafts at the water's surface. The air reaches the divers through a long, thin hose. Snuba divers can also use motorized engines to travel around the shallow waters.

❸ **Seawalking**
Underwater helmets are all that is needed for a walk along the seabed. The Underwater Helmet Diving System is an innovative invention allowing the amount of air necessary for normal breathing to be delivered to the helmet. Air circulates within the weighted helmet and the diver breathes as normal. Seawalking is most common in the warm waters of the southern hemisphere.

❹ **Hydropolis hotel**
The world's first underwater hotel is currently being built 65 ft (20 m) beneath the surface of the Arabian Gulf in Dubai. Held in place by 7,000 anchors, Hydropolis consists of a land station where guests arrive, a connecting tunnel to transport people to the main hotel block, and 220 underwater suites. The hotel is expected to cost $550 million to build.

2,000 ft
(600 m)

2,500 ft
(750 m)

4,000 ft
(1,200 m)

Sperm whale

14,000 ft
(4,267 m)

30,000 ft
(8,500 m)

Deep-sea fish

37,729 ft
(11,500 m)

5 Scuba

During the 1940s, Self-Contained Underwater Breathing Apparatus (SCUBA) was invented. Divers could carry their own supply of compressed air in tanks on their backs. Using scuba equipment, marine biologists can observe creatures in their natural environment.

6 Free-diving

For this type of diving, people train to hold their breath for sustained periods while underwater. Competitive free-diving is regarded as an extreme sport because divers go to great depths on one single breath. A weighted sled is used to help the diver descend and a buoyancy aid assists with the ascent.

7 Newt suit

Thick-walled, cast aluminum suits can withstand huge pressure deep underwater. Joints in the arms and legs allow the diver to move easily. The suit provides up to eight hours of air. These suits are mainly used in oil exploration—the diver inspects the oil platform through the viewing bubble.

8 Deep-Sea Rescue Vehicle

The British, Swedish, and US navies have all built Deep-Sea Rescue Vehicles (DSRV), which can help to save the trapped crew if a submarine sinks. The rescue vehicles are attached to ships on the surface and released in the event of an emergency. Here, the US *Avalon* rescue vehicle is being prepared for a mission.

9 *Alvin*

US-manned submersible *Alvin* entered service in 1964 and has been on more than 3,000 dives. *Alvin's* achievements include locating a hydrogen bomb on the bed of the Mediterranean Sea, discovering giant tubeworms in the Pacific Ocean, and visiting the wreck of the *Titanic*.

10 *Trieste*

A bathyscaphe is a deep-sea vessel comprising a flotation hull with a manned observation chamber. On January 23, 1960, the bathyscaphe *Trieste* traveled down to the deepest point on the planet—the Marianas Trench in the Pacific Ocean. Built to resist pressure of 200,000 tons, *Trieste* is the only vessel to achieve this.

Submarine

Nuclear-powered submarines can stay at sea for months at a time without resurfacing. The nuclear power provides an unlimited source of heat to turn water into steam, allowing submarines to travel long distances at high speed. This has revolutionized sea warfare, with nuclear submarines such as the US Navy's Seawolf-class able to reach depths of more than 1,970 ft (600 m) and travel around the world without refueling. Today, the only limitation to time spent at sea is the food supply on board.

SEAWOLF (SSN-21) CLASS

This class of submarine is larger, faster, quieter, and more expensive than any submarine to date. For shallow water missions, each vessel has a floodable chamber called a silo used to place eight divers and their equipment into water.

Specifications:	
Length	354 ft (108 m)
Width	39 ft (12 m)
Speed	40 mph (65 km/h)
Depth (min)	36 ft (11 m)
Depth (max)	1,970 ft (600 m)
Power	S6W nuclear reactor
Crew	133 (12 officers, 121 sailors)

Weapons room
In its double-deck weapons room, a Seawolf-class submarine is equipped to carry tomahawk cruise missiles, harpoon missiles, torpedoes, and mines. The torpedoes can be launched via one of eight torpedo tubes on board. The well equipped weapons room allows the submarine to respond to military threats from other submarines, ships, and even air attacks.

Driving force
The control room of a modern submarine resembles an aircraft's flight deck. The submarine "pilots" must control the angle and depth of the vessel to keep it straight and level. The submarine can maneuver at high speed and extreme angles, but restraining straps keep the crew safely in their seats.

Life on board
Ventilation, air purification systems, and a substantial freshwater supply for drinking and bathing are all features of modern submarines. The multideck Seawolf-class submarines offer more spacious sleeping quarters than smaller vessels, in which sailors sleep between racks of torpedoes. When off duty, submariners can play computer games and watch movies.

Aircraft carrier

Aircraft carriers are among the world's largest ships, able to support a crew of more than 6,000. The Nimitz class of modern nuclear-powered supercarriers is the largest of all and includes the USS *George Washington*. Launched in 1990, the carrier is 1,093 ft (333 m) long, 256 ft (78 m) wide, and the same height as a 24-story building. Although it could travel for 18 years without refueling, most missions only last a few months.

Bridge The supercarrier is steered from a forward-facing bridge. Navigation facilities for the captain are also found here.

Operations room Staff constantly monitor live screen pictures of the comings and goings on the flight deck. They also use radar systems to survey the air space above the carrier.

Engine controls The carrier has two nuclear reactors, which are controlled remotely from this base.

Briefing room The pilots have meetings and debriefings in this room. There is a seat specifically for each pilot. The headrest of every seat is marked with the call sign of an individual pilot.

Primary flight control The tricky takeoffs and landings are coordinated from this position overlooking the flight deck.

The air boss is in charge of monitoring proceedings and taking action when a takeoff or landing is proving a problem.

Takeoff The runway is only 298 ft (91 m) long, so huge acceleration is needed to clear it. Planes must have a lot of air moving over the wings at takeoff. The carrier plows through water to increase the airflow and catapults are used to speed planes up.

Island superstructure This area is the central core of the carrier, housing the bridge, primary flight control center, and air traffic control center. The Island is decorated with awards for excellence.

Helicopter In case of an emergency, such as an aircraft falling over the side, the carrier's helicopters are on hand to assist.

Weapons The aircraft on board include fighter, strike, and transport planes. They carry a variety of weapons, such as

The carrier is powered for a year on a piece of fuel the same size as a soda can!

 Pumping fuel In the pump room, fuel (known as "JP5") for the aircraft and other engines is filtered and pumped up to the flight deck. There is a laboratory on board where the JP5 fuel is regularly analyzed for consistency.

Bakery The chefs knead the dough before cooking it in the ovens. Each day, hundreds of loaves are freshly baked.

 Cafeteria The enormous cafeteria caters to the crew of 6,000 men and women three times a day.

Gym A state-of-the-art gym is essential to ensure the crew stays fit enough to carry out the demanding onboard procedures.

 Deck crew The flight deck is patrolled by officers who use radio communication to help guide the planes around the carrier.

 Catapult control This is a retractable pod where crew involved in the takeoff of aircraft can view the deck, while staying at a safe distance.

Catapult This is one of four steam-powered catapults, used to get planes to high speeds over a very short distance.

Preparing for takeoff A Hawkeye aircraft is secured to a catapult system that will project it quickly into the air.

Signaling takeoff When giving clearance for takeoff, crew members wear helmets called "cranials" to block out engine noise.

Landing Every plane has a tailhook. To stop quickly, the pilot must hook this on to one of four wires laid out on the carrier deck.

 Arresting An aircraft picks up one of four wires with its tailhook, and comes to an abrupt halt. This is called "arresting." If an aircraft misses the wires, the pilot takes off again and attempts another landing. This practice is called "touch and go."

bombs, rockets, guided missiles, and torpedoes. These are used on air, sea, and land missions.

 Propeller shaft A crewman checks a shaft driving one of the supercarrier's four giant propellers.

Maintenance In the engine-maintenance bay, aircraft undergo routine checks. If there is a serious technical problem, the aircraft is grounded until the fault is fixed.

 Aircraft hangar When the carrier's 85 aircraft are not in use or on the flight deck, they are stored in the hangar. Servicing crews regularly check and maintain them. The hangar is three decks high and has four massive lifts to maneuver the planes and spare parts to and from the flight deck.

Mechanics of sailing

Dinghy sailing is a thrilling sport, but it requires training, skill, and determination. First, a sailor must understand how the boat works. A sailboat harnesses the power of the wind in its sails and uses this to move in a particular direction. The boat's four main parts are the hull, keel, sails, and rudder. The hull is the body of the boat. It keeps the water out, holds the mast, and provides somewhere for the crew to sit. The keel is a beam that runs along the bottom of the hull and prevents the boat from being blown sideways. There

are usually two sails and these are attached to a mast. A sailor must fine-tune the position of the sails almost constantly, aiming to keep the wind flowing over them as smoothly as possible. The rudder is integral to steering the boat. It is a flat piece of material, such as wood or fiberglass, that projects from part of the stern (back) of the boat into the water. The rudder is moved left or right using a lever called a tiller. It does not take long to learn the parts of a boat and the basic principles of sailing, but it takes years to become an experienced sailor, ready to meet any challenge at sea.

Rigging and ropes
The mast is held up by a mesh of ropes known as rigging. There is a pole jutting out from the bottom of the mast to support the sail and this is called the boom. Rectangular sails have another pole, known as a yard, at the top. The ropes for adjusting the sails are called sheets. All the ropes tie on to fittings called cleats.

Points of sailing
Wind moving past a sail produces a force at right angles to the sail. Adjusting the sail takes the boat in different directions, known as the points of sailing. A sailboat can travel in any direction except straight into the wind (the no-go zone). The only way around it is to take a zigzag course—this is called tacking.

Mainsail, Batton, Mast, Rigging, Boom, Stern, Hull, Rudder, Tiller, Gunwhales, Side deck, Cleat, Jib sail, Fore deck, Bow

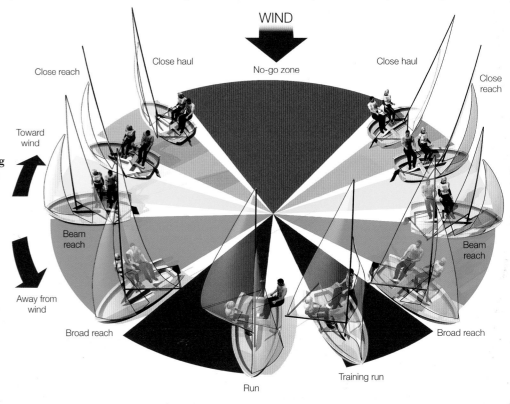

WIND, No-go zone, Close haul, Close reach, Toward wind, Beam reach, Away from wind, Broad reach, Run, Training run

Balancing the boat

Sailors can use their own bodies to counteract the force of the wind and keep the boat as upright in the water as possible. The sailing team consists of a helmsman, who makes key decisions and controls onboard procedures, together with a support crew of at least one person. The team on this racing dinghy is standing on the gunwhales—the top edge of the side of the boat. They lean out of the windward side, pulling against the billowing sails.

TACKING: SAILING TOWARD THE WIND

Turning so that the bow (front) of the boat passes through the wind is called tacking. Taking a series of zigzag turns allows the boat to reach a part of the no-go zone.

WIND

1. The helmsman and crew member sit forward. The helmsman controls the mainsheet (rope to adjust the mainsail) and tiller. The crew member controls the jib sheet.

2. The helmsman calls "lee-oh!" and pushes the tiller toward the sail. The crew member releases the jib sheet. Both move to the center. As the boat turns, the crew member lifts the other jib sheet to fill the sails.

3. The helmsman moves the tiller to central and trims the sails—this involves pulling on the sheets to adjust the sail positions. Both helmsman and crew member sit back to balance the boat.

GYBING: SAILING AWAY FROM THE WIND

Turning so that the stern (back) of the boat passes through the wind is called gybing. In strong winds, the turn is extremely quick, but in light winds, the boat turns through a slow, wide arc.

WIND

1. Gybing is a tricky maneuver. Before starting the turn, the helmsman checks that the boat is balanced, the area is clear, and the main sheet is hauled in tight.

2. The helmsman and crew member move to the boat's center. The helmsman calls "gybe-oh!" and ducks as the boom starts to swing across the stern. As it reaches the center, the helmsman centers the tiller.

3. The helmsman and crew member shift their weight to the new windward side of the boat. The crew member adjusts the jib sail, known as "trimming the jib".

Main halyard storage elastic

Boom strap

Wing bar end elastic

Mainsheet leash

Spinnaker block elastic

Spinnaker block ties

Control block ties

Kicker block tie

Lead weight

Mainsheet pad eyes

Front wing "U" bolt

Assorted hardware

Spinnaker pole rear strap

Bobbles

Micro cleat fairlead

Hull

Spinnaker bag

Spinnaker

Cable ties

Daggerboard

Rear wing "U" bolts

Deck loop

Wing bar nonslip tape

Control line rings

Mast step

Front spinnaker pole "U" bolts

Building the boat

Built to order, the hull of RS Racing's RS700 is a composite of fiberglass and foam, which keeps it both strong and lightweight. Once the hull has been thoroughly checked and any imperfections repaired, the other parts of the boat, including the mast, sails, and rigging, are attached. The hull has exactly 100 tiny holes through which the assorted fittings are secured. It takes about two days to fully assemble an RS700.

Tie

Control block ties

Wing elbows

Wire-kicking strap

Wing bar end ties

Downhaul

Spin chute elastic

Daggerboard leash

Strong sails

The fabric of the RS700 sails is reinforced with the material Kevlar®, which is stronger than steel and prevents ripping or snagging. The spinnaker (balloonlike sail, forward of the mainsail) is protected by a water-repellent silicone coating. Kevlar® and silicone give the sails a much longer life at sea before they must be replaced.

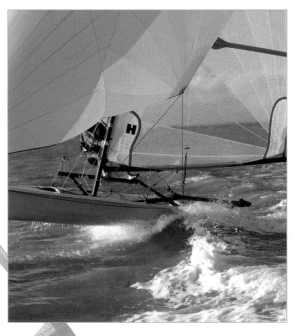

Balancing act

In light winds, the RS700 stays flat with no danger of keeling over. When the wind picks up, the sailor must use his or her body weight to balance the boat. In strong winds, any skiff with large sails needs a trapeze to stay balanced. A trapeze is a rope connected to the mast, allowing the sailor to suspend him or herself out of the boat. This counteracts the effect of the wind while maintaining racing speed.

Ideal for solo sailing, the RS700 skiff (shallow boat) was designed with racing in mind. The size and weight of the sailor was previously a factor in racing—the lighter and smaller the sailor, the faster the boat powered through the waves. The RS700's performance equalization system eliminates this. Adjustable "wings" (beams attached to the hull) are extended or narrowed to ensure that all sailors have the same height advantage, and a lead track with weights makes the load of each boat identical. With the race fair, anyone can be a winner!

Racing sailboat

Fast moves

In a single-handed racing skiff, everything must be easy for the solo sailor to reach and operate. The simple design of the RS700 allows the sailor to take up a secure central position behind the mast and move freely around the boat. The ropes are clearly color-coded, allowing the sailor to quickly identify which one operates the mainsail, spinnaker, or boom (sail support), without wasting time during a race.

Dry hull

The long, pointed shape of the hull (vessel frame) helps the RS700 move faster in water. Although the hull weighs only 123 lb (56 kg), it is strong and stable. Very little seawater can enter the hull. If the boat goes through a wave, the open deck at the bow (front) is designed to shed any excess water quickly. This means race entrants can keep their speed up without surplus water slowing them down.

Trapeze adjuster rope

Outhaul control line

Center strap

Pintle

Low-friction tape

Gudgen

Micro air blocks with swivel

Open vernier adjusters

Mainsheet swivel

1.6-in (4-cm) shackle

Spinnaker sheet ratchet block

Tuffnel pads

Spinnaker halyard takeup

1.6-in (4-cm) carbo blocks

Spinnaker sheet

Mainsheet

Shroud adjuster

Rack bearing set

Cunningham control line

Spinnaker halyard

Micro double block

1.6-in (4-cm) Carbo blocks with spring and deck loop

Rudder retaining clip

Rudder stock and tiller

Mainsheet ratchet block

Rudder

Kicker control line

Wide trapeze ring

Boom

1 **Bowman** Agility is required in this action-packed role. The bowman must handle the triangular spinnaker sail and prepare other sails for raising.

2 **Sail store** The weather conditions and wind speed dictate choice of sail. This is where sails are stored until they are required for use.

3 **Sewerman** The wet, dark sail store is nicknamed the sewer. The sewerman is in charge of packing and organizing the sails, and stays in the store during the race.

4 **Midbowman** On deck, the midbowman works alongside the bowman, mastman, and pitman to administer sail changes, including to the spinnaker and poles.

5 **Mastman** Together with the pitman, the mastman uses weight and strength to hoist the sails as the grinders take up the slack.

6 **Pitman** Responsible for the front section of the boat, the pitman goes into the pit to help with the ropes around the mast. This role also involves assisting the grinders.

7 **Grinder** When the boat sails toward or away from the wind, huge sudden bursts of strength are required from the grinders to power the winches that trim (set) the sails.

8 **Grinder** Sails are hoisted and trimmed by running ropes around mechanical winches. The grinders power these winches in response to the trimmers' demands.

9 **Trimmer** The trimmers control the spinnaker downwind and the headsail upwind. They help the skipper to decide the best speed.

10 **Trimmer** Experienced trimmers can generate increased speed from their yacht as the situation dictates, even before computers on board can detect it.

11 **Mainsail grinder** The biggest winch on the yacht is the one controlling the mainsail, and manning this is the mainsail grinder's major task.

12 **Traveler** With the assistance of the mainsail trimmer, the traveler trims the mainsail, as well as keeping track of the speed upwind.

13 **Mainsail trimmer** With a sound knowledge of sails and rigging, this type of trimmer controls the ropes that shape the mainsail to generate maximum performance.

14 **Navigator** In charge of the vessel's computers and electronic instruments, the navigator relays weather and route information to the team.

15 **Skipper** The public face of the team, the skipper is responsible for steering the boat, motivating the team, and ultimately, the safety of all on board.

16 **Strategist** The strategist looks out for changes in weather and the wind's speed and direction as these will affect the remainder of the course.

17 **Tactician** As the eyes of the boat, the tactician oversees the boat's tactical position in relation to opposition yachts, wind, and current.

18 **Runner** The rigging that holds tension in the mast must be adjusted every time the boat changes course. The runner controls this with a winch.

All hands on deck

The America's Cup races are short, so there is no accommodation on board for the crew. The deck is crowded with crew, so each person has to stay focused on their individual tasks. The crew must pull together to tackle difficult maneuvers, high winds, or choppy seas.

Crafting the cup

Inscribed in silver on the ornate America's Cup trophy are the names of all the yachts that have taken part in the race—both winners and challengers. In order to make room for more names, silver bases were introduced and placed under the cup in 1958 and 2001.

Superyacht

New for the 21st century, the 118 WallyPower is the ultimate superyacht. This privately owned, luxury yacht combines the latest engineering with futuristic design. The 118-ft (36-m) motor-powered boat is packed with high-tech systems and luxurious fixtures, concealed beneath a sleek, clean exterior. Weighing 95 tons and cruising at 68 mph (110 km/h), 118 WallyPower has a professional crew and room for six guests to enjoy the high life on the high seas.

Launch boat
A panel in the front deck opens hydraulically to reveal the garage. Inside, an 18-ft (5.5-m) dinghy, known as a tender, is housed. If the guests want to go ashore, a crane launches the tender into the water. When the teak-floor garage is empty, it is used as a gym.

Navigation station
The navigation area resembles a flight deck more than a boat's control center. This console is used for the startup, engineering, and monitoring systems. Two other consoles control the steering, communication, and navigation.

Type: Fast motor yacht   **Year built**: 2002   **Shipyard**: Intermarine-Rodriquez, Italy   **Maximum power**: 16,800 HP   **Fuel tank capacity**: 22,000 liters   **Maximum width**: 24 ft (7.4 m)   **Accommodation**: 6 guests, 6 crew

oft-style lounge

ccessed through an automatic sliding door,
e spacious, open lounge area has teak floors,
ft cushions, and views through the tinted
ass windows. On hot days, when the boat is
nchored, this is the coolest part of the vessel.

Diving platform

The two side decks along the superstructure are
protected by bulwarks—raised sections above deck.
At anchor, these bulwarks drop down hydraulically
to increase light, enhance the view, and serve as
diving platforms.

Sea view

The superstructure of 118 WallyPower consists
of a carbon frame, covered with glass panels.
All the doors and windows open automatically.
From the inside, guests have a 360-degree
panoramic view. Outside, a metallic paint
coating changes the color and appearance of
the boat, depending on light and location.

Superstructure: Carbon fiber and laminated composite glass   **Draught (depth below surface)**: 4.5 ft (1.36 m)   **Deck finish**: Teak

Speed tests

The vessel had to undergo extensive
testing to ensure its innovative hull
design was suited to traveling at
top speeds of 81 mph (130 km/h).
The engines had to be versatile
enough to travel at high and low
speeds, and in calm and rough seas.
Three gas turbine motors drive the
waterjets to achieve the top speed in
open water, while two diesel engines
power the waterjets for slow sailing
in narrow waters.

Profile plan

Navigation cockpit

Lounge area   Dining area   Bedroom   Dinghy

Lower layout

Dinghy

Engine room   Galley   Bedroom

Below deck

The navigation cockpit, diner, and
lounge are one continuous, open-plan
space. Under the dining area, a skylight
illuminates the lower deck. This deck
has a vast, sound-proofed engine room
where the two diesel engines and three
gas turbines are located. The next
compartment is the galley (kitchen),
followed by the bedrooms with en-suite
bathrooms for the guests and the crew.

Cruising

Before air travel became widely available, the ocean liner was the only way to cross oceans and visit other continents. Even today, there is no other way to reach Antarctica. During the early 20th century, liners became famous for the luxury they offered to the highest-paying passengers. There was elegant dining, glittering entertainment, and extravagant balls. Luxury is still one of the main attractions of cruise ships, together with visits to exotic ports en route.

New horizons

In the past, ocean liners were a form of transportation for passengers traveling from one destination to another, with luxurious rooms for high-paying first-class passengers and basic cabins for second- and third-class passengers. Although aircraft now have the monopoly on long-distance travel, ocean liners have evolved to become a vacation experience in themselves. Passengers on modern cruise ships enjoy a wide range of on-board facilities, as well as short stops at interesting ports along the way.

On-board dip

Swimming for fun and relaxation became very popular during the 1930s. Cruise liners built in that decade usually had one small indoor pool to satisfy the demand. Today's ships offer a selection of facilities, including indoor and outdoor pools, jacuzzis, saunas, and steam rooms.

Stylish surroundings

Cruise ship interiors have always reflected the fashions and designs of the day. In the 1930s, the dominant look was Art Deco, featuring chrome pillars, lights, mirrors, and gilt. Modern interiors use lightweight, durable materials and styles are more minimalist with clean, functional lines.

Luxury accommodation

Cabins are graded according to their amenities, with the more expensive accommodation offering sea views or balconies, fresh flowers and fruit, and even butler service. Today, there are extra facilities, including a telephone, television, refrigerator, and en suite bathroom.

Fitness on deck

Many early liners were not equipped with exercise facilities so passengers used to take a walk around the deck to stretch their legs. There are many more options available today, with passengers participating in regular fitness classes or using state-of-the-art indoor gyms.

Entertainment options

From jazz bands to symphony orchestras, music was the top form of cruise ship entertainment in the past. There were also deck games, such as donkey derbies and a throwing game called quoits. Now ships have movie theaters, theaters, casinos, libraries, dance floors, and bingo.

Dining experience

Formal dining characterized the cruise ship experience, with men wearing black tie, women wearing evening gowns, and chefs serving up fine cuisine. Many modern liners offer self-service buffets as well as waiter service. Other informal dining options include cafés, pubs, and poolside bars.

Modern cruises

Several hundred cruise ships are operating around the world today. Their itineraries range from round-the-world trips to mini-breaks around the Mediterranean or Caribbean seas. Other popular destinations include tiny islands in the Pacific Ocean and the scenic Scandinavian fjords.

Luxury liner

Welcome on board the *Queen Mary 2*. Launched in 2004, this enormous cruise liner is the same length as 41 double-decker buses and can carry 2,620 passengers. The vessel spends summers in European waters, while winters are passed across the Atlantic, cruising around the Americas and Canada. The *Queen Mary 2* is expected to sail for 40 years, traveling the equivalent of 12 trips to the Moon.

1 Guests in the Royal Suites dine at the Queen's Grill. The menu changes each evening, but meals can also be made specially to customers' request.

2 This is one of five saltwater swimming pools dotted around the ship in various shapes and sizes. Each has a pool bar for drinks and snacks.

3 The nightclub, G32, has a huge dance floor. Rock and hip-hop music is played most nights. During the day, ballroom dancing classes take place.

4 Named after the leading US chef, the Todd English restaurant is a favorite with food critics. Mediterranean cuisine is served inside or alfresco.

5 Past luxury of classic cruise liners is relived in the ornate, three-story Britannia restaurant, also home to the largest wine cellar at sea.

6 An audio tour, called the Maritime Quest Exhibit, takes passengers back to the golden era of cruising using photographs and wall panels.

7 Children are entertained in the Play Zone. This well-run camp has toys, boardgames, computer terminals, and a splash pool.

8 In an emergency, there are 14 semi-enclosed lifeboats and eight tender lifeboats, each for 150 people, plus two fast six-person rescue boats.

9 This traditional English pub, The Golden Lion, offers drinks, bar food, karaoke, and televised sports events.

10 The Veuve Clicquot bar serves champagne in fine Waterford flute glasses. A selection of coffees and pastries are available.

11 Roulette wheels, fruit machines, card tables, and dice games are all on show at the exclusive, late-night Empire casino.

12 From evening gowns to sportswear, passengers can enjoy browsing and buying at the Mayfair shopping area.

WINCH ONLY

19

15

17

16

18

20

21

22

23

24

CUNARD

Queen Mary 2

SUPERSIZE SPECIFICATIONS

The *Queen Mary 2* has 14 decks of sports facilities, bars, shops, cabins, and lounges, as well as 10 restaurants. The height of the vessel is about the same as that of a 23-story building, while the power room could light a small city. From a distance, the vessel is as easy to hear as it is to spot—the whistle is audible 10 miles (16 km) away!

Cost: $1 billion	
Length: 1,132 ft (345 m)	
Width: 135 ft (41 m)	
Height (keel to funnel): 236 ft (72 m)	
Speed: 34 mph (55 km/h)	
Power: 157,000 horsepower engines	
Passengers: 2,620	
Crew: 1,253	

13 In the Grand Lobby, a classical-style staircase, surrounded by cabins on either side, leads down to luxurious seating and modern works of art.

14 The King's Court comprises four restaurants—Asian, Italian, a carvery, and the chef's galley, where guests can watch their meals being prepared.

15 Flowers bloom throughout the year at the colonial-style Winter Garden, while a string quartet adds to the relaxing ambience.

16 A variety of plays, operas, musicals, readings, and live acts are shown at the Royal Court Theater. Workshops and drama classes are held for guests.

17 The Canyon Ranch Spa Club is the biggest on any ship. There are 24 treatment rooms, a thermal suite, reflexology basins, and a steam room.

18 The ship has a lecture program, ConneXions, where topical issues are presented and discussed with experts from leading international institutions.

19 Activities available at the sports center include a golf driving range, playing field, and a state-of-the-art gym with a separate weight room.

20 This floating planetarium is called Illuminations. It also functions as a movie theater, 500-seat lecture hall, and broadcasting studio.

21 All the rooms of the Royal Suites have private lift access, whirlpool baths, walk-in closets, en-suite bars, fresh flowers, and 24-hour room service.

22 At the Commodore Club, cocktails are served while live jazz is played against a background panorama of the night sky.

23 This is the world's largest library at sea and guests can learn more about lecture subjects here. A bookstore is located next door.

24 Dotted all around the ship are more than 300 works of art valued at $5.4 million. Well-known artists were commissioned to create them.

Switch
The driver presses a button to start the four-second transformation into a marine vehicle. Gibbs Aquada cuts the drive to the wheels, which retract to prevent dragging. The trim tabs (rear plates) adjust to help lift the boat out of the water.

On Land
Gibbs Aquada performs like a sports car, accelerating from 0–60 mph (0–96 kph) in under 10 seconds and traveling at speeds of up to 100 mph (160 kph). However, to prevent water leaks, there are no doors, so the driver must climb into the vehicle.

Aquada

Making waves in the world of high-tech, high-performance leisure vehicles is the dual-purpose Gibbs Aquada, equipped to race on roads and cruise in water. At the press of a button, Gibbs Aquada automatically makes the transition from moving on land to working in water. This award-winning vehicle was launched in 2003, after seven years of planning and the efforts of more than 70 engineers and designers. In the future, the vehicle's creators—Gibbs Technologies Ltd—hopes to introduce its high-speed water-traversing technology to other types of motor vehicle.

In Water
The same engine that moved Gibbs Aquada on land now provides power to the vehicle's submerged jet. The jet begins expelling water to propel Gibbs Aquada through the water at speeds of 30 mph (48 km/h). A water skier can even be towed behind the vehicle!

Interior features

Gibbs Aquada's dashboard displays show marine and land speeds, as well as mileage. The seats are made of fully waterproof marine vinyl, and the central seating improves passenger weight distribution on water, especially if the driver is alone. A storage net underneath each seat carries a life jacket.

Technical specifications

On the road
6 ft 7 in (2.05 m) 15 ft 9 in (4.81 m)

In the water
26 in (650 mm) max 12 in (300 mm)

Category	Private Light Vehicle and RCD
Engine	175 hp, 24 valve, V6, 0.5 gallons (2.5 liter)
Gearbox	5-speed auto and reverse
Fuel capacity	15 gallons (67 liters) of 95 Ron Unleaded
Completed	2003
Anticorrosion	To marine standards
Seating	Three elevated seats
Jet	2,072 lb (940 kg) thrust
Vehicle weight	3,232 lb (1,466 kg)
Buoyancy	Nonsinkable if swamped
Top speeds	Water 30 mph (48 km/h), land 100 mph (160 km/h)
Lights	Road and marine navigation lights

Aquabatic achievements

- In 1999, the greatest swim in white water was performed by American Thom Stanton. He swam through 7 miles (12 km) of dangerous, fast-moving rapids.

- The largest wave successfully surfed was 70 ft (21.3 m) in height. It was ridden in 2004 by American Pete Cabrinha at a place known as "Jaws" (Peahi) on Maui in Hawaii.

- In 2005, American George Blair became the oldest water-skier when he water-skied across Lake Florence in Florida at aged 90.

- American kite surfers Fabrice Collard, Kent Marincovik, and Neil Hutchinson made the longest continuous kite-surfing journey when they traveled 101 miles (163 km) from Key West to Cuba in 1991.

- In 2000, Englishman Shaun Baker made the fastest-ever canoe descent when he descended a vertical height of 75 ft (22.8 m) in 19.9 seconds on a river in Wales.

- The record for most people riding a wave on a surfboard at one time was achieved by a 14-strong team in Cornwall, England, on July 22, 2003. The giant surfboard measured a staggering 37 ft (11 m).

Surfing

The first recorded document to describe surfing dates back to the 18th century. After the death of explorer Captain Cook in 1779, Lieutenant James King completed Cook's journals and included observations of surfing with a narrow board. Competitive surfing is very popular, but searching for the biggest waves, known as "rhino hunting," is also a favorite pursuit. When a surfer is knocked over by a wave, it is called a "wipeout."

Aquabatics

Watersports have been gaining popularity since the 1950s, when surfing first took off and the mass production of pleasure boats began. A combination of classic watersports and imaginative new craft means the oceans are alive with adventure and activity, as people find ever more exciting ways to ride the waves.

Windsurfing
This wind-powered sport began in the 1960s in the US and became an Olympic event in 1984. By the 1990s, its popularity waned, as the equipment became too specialized and complicated to use. Recently, the development of basic board and sail designs, aimed at beginners, has renewed interest in windsurfing.

Kayaking
The Inuit, an Arctic people, developed the kayak, meaning "man's boat." It is similar to a canoe, but single-paddled and sealed, so, if the kayak overturns, water will not leak inside. The first kayaks were made of wood covered in sealskin. Fiberglass, carbon, and plastic are used today.

Jet skiing
First invented in the 1970s, these engine-propelled craft use jets to expel water and can travel at speeds of 37 mph (60 km/h). Modern jet skis are equipped with a lanyard—a switch to cut the engine if the rider falls. Jet skis are gaining in popularity as they are relatively cheap to buy and give the owner freedom to ride the seas.

Dragon boat racing
About 2,500 years ago, dragon boat racing began in southern China and has since spread across the world. The boats are decorated with dragon heads at the bow and tails at the stern. The standard crew of 22 consists of 10 pairs of paddlers, a steerer, and a drummer, whose beating dictates the timing of the paddle strokes.

Kite surfing
This sport developed from surfing. A surfer, attached to a board, maneuvers a kite in the wind and gets carried along. In strong winds on calm water, a kite-surfer can travel at speeds of 31 mph (50 km/h). "Airtime" refers to how long a kite-surfer is lifted clean out of the water. The record stands at 8.9 seconds!

White water rafting
Turbulent river waves are known as white water. A six-tier classification system exists to inform rafters of the difficulty of each river. Class one means easy to navigate, but class six carries the risk of death! Manageable rapids in South America and Canada are the most popular.

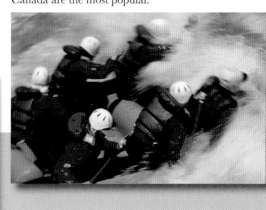

River boats

Over the centuries, all kinds of vessels have been built for traveling along inland waterways. River boats may have to contend with sand banks or hidden rocks, so they often have a shallow hull. The exact design depends on local materials and how the boat will be used, for example, short fishing trips or transporting heavy goods. Some river boats are complete mobile homes, with a galley (kitchen) and berths for sleeping.

Plank boats

In the state of Kerala, in southwestern India, people make huge boats called kettuvalams. Some are 82 ft (25 m) long. Constructed from wooden planks, each tied to the next with coir (coconut) rope, the boats were traditionally used to transport rice, coconuts, and spices. Today, many have been converted into houseboats for tourists.

Floating markets

Early in the mornings, Thailand's floating markets open for trade on rivers and canals. Sellers arrive in boats laden with vegetables, flowers, and fruits. The boats stay near the water's edge, so customers on land can view the goods. The largest floating market is in Ratchaburi, 50 miles (80 km) southwest of Bangkok.

City of gondolas

The Italian city of Venice is built on a series of islands linked by 150 canals. There are no roads for cars, so the only way to travel is on foot or by boat. Venice is known for its long, narrow gondolas, rowed by gondoliers, but ordinary Venetians usually travel by *vaporetto* (water bus).

High-altitude homes

Lying more than 12,467 ft (3,800 m) above sea level, Lake Titicaca in the Andes mountains is the world's highest navigable (deep enough for boats) lake. The Uros Indians live there on islands built from a reed called totora. Their boats are made from the same material. The Uros use the boats to hunt ducks, fish in the lake, and visit islands nearby.

Full steam ahead

The Mississippi River, which flows through the southern US, is famous for its paddle steamers. They are powered by a steam engine, which drives a paddle wheel. As the wheel turns, the paddles push through the water and the boat moves forward. Some steamers are floating museums or casinos, but most carry tourists on trips.

Busy with barges

Amsterdam, in the Netherlands, has about 2,500 houseboats along its numerous canals. Many boats are former Dutch barges, which were originally built to carry freight and have since been converted into homes. Along the city's Singel Canal, a regular flower market is held on the barges.

Bridges

Spanning rivers and canals, bridges provide a passage for people to cross. Although many bridges are fixed structures, sometimes they must be moveable to allow people to pass over and boats to go underneath. Depending on the design, a bridge may lift, swing, tilt, fold, curl up, or even sink!

Going up
The Falkirk Wheel in central Scotland connects two canals that have a height difference of 115 ft (35 m). In the past, barges had to pass through 11 locks to get between levels, but now the rotating wheel lifts them instead.

Going down
Instead of raising its deck to allow boats through, a submersible bridge lowers into the water. There is a submersible bridge at either end of the Corinth Canal in Greece. To let boats pass, each one sinks to the bottom of the 26-ft- (8-m-) deep canal.

The upper gondola carries barges to the Forth and Clyde Canal.

The gondola holds four 66-ft (20-m) barges. Cogs keep it level at all times.

The arm turns on a central cog attached to the aqueduct support.

Aqueduct support

Hanging platform

Known as a transporter bridge, this structure crosses the Nervión River in Spain. A gondola (platform) for cars hangs on long wires from its extremely high span. This gondola is moved across the river by traction when no ships are passing under. Only about 20 transporter bridges were ever built, and just eight are still in use.

Reinforced concrete aqueduct (water channel) leads to the Union Canal.

Gondola is held by wires, attached to wheels on tracks, that span the bridge.

Folding bridge

The Hörnbrücke is a folding footbridge in Kiel, northern Germany. It was built in 1997 to take passengers from the city center to the ferry port. Every hour, the Hörnbrücke folds into the shape of the letter "N" so large vessels can pass through and up the Hörn River.

Tilting bridge

Built to carry foot traffic and cyclists, the Gateshead Millennium Bridge spans the Tyne River in northeastern England. Two hydraulic pumps provide the power to tilt the bridge. As the top arch tilts lower, the pathway rises and makes room for boats underneath.

One-minute wonder

Completed in 1893, London's Tower Bridge can be raised in just one minute to allow tall ships to pass under it. The bridge still uses the original hydraulic system to lift the bridge halves, or bascules. The bridge is raised about 900 times every year.

Smallest submarine
In 1991, English engineer William Smith built the world's tiniest submarine, *Water Beatle*. At just 9 ft 7 in (2.95 m) long, 3 ft 8 in (1.15 m) wide, and 4 ft 7 in (1.42 m) high, *Water Beatle* is smaller than a Mini car. It has three air cylinders, allowing it to stay underwater for more than four hours.

Biggest boat tie-up
At the 2003 Raft-Off Regatta on Lake Norman, in North Carolina, 944 boats were tied together in a continual free-floating line.

Largest hovercraft
The British SRN4 MK II hovercraft is 184 ft (56 m) in length and weighs 310 tons. On board, there is room for 418 passengers and 60 cars. The hovercraft's top speed is 75 mph (120 km/h).

Longest pedal-boat journey
Between October 1992 and February 1993, Japanese record-breaker Kenichi Horie traveled from Hawaii to Okinawa in Japan by pedal boat. It took him almost four months to cover the distance of 4,660 miles (7,500 km).

Largest propeller
Japanese Shipbuilders Stone Manganese Marine Ltd. designed and manufactured a giant six-bladed propeller. It has a width of 29.5 ft (9 m) and weighs a hefty 93.5 tons.

Longest canal
China's Grand Canal connects Hang Zhou in the south to Beijing in the north. First constructed by manual laborers in 283 CE, it was rebuilt between 1958–72 to a length of 1,115 miles (1,795 km).

Fastest propeller-driven boat
In 2004, off the coast of California, American David Villwock achieved a record-breaking speed of 220 mph (355 km/h) in a hydroplane.

Greatest car-carrier
The ferry *Ulysses*, belonging to Irish Ferries, was launched in 2000. Not only is there room for 1,342 cars, but it can also carry a staggering 59,925 passengers, too.

Water records

The challenge of choppy seas, strong currents, and severe gales is not enough for some sailors and watersports enthusiasts. Instead, they are busy making a huge splash in the record books by such feats as constructing the world's biggest sail, largest yacht, and smallest submarine, as well as pedaling a tiny boat across a vast ocean.

Land

Timeline

MODEL OF EARLY WHEEL

The wheel
The first wheel is made from three planks pegged together and cut into a circle. These heavy, solid wheels are fitted onto axles with pegs and are used to carry the first carts.

EARLY PUBLIC BUS

Public bus
The first horse-drawn public bus is introduced in Paris, France, by inventor Blaise Pascal. The bus service has a regular route, timetable, and fare system.

LONDON UNDERGROUND SIGN

Underground rail
The world's first underground rail service is introduced in London. The noisy, steam-powered railroad runs for 3.7 miles (6 km) across the city.

EARLY DUTCH TRAM

Electric trams
The first electric tram is built by German engineer Werner von Siemens in Berlin. Cities around the world replace their horse-hauled tramways with electric systems.

GRUNER TAXIMETER

Fairer fares
German Wilhelm Bruhn invents the modern taximeter. The device is used to measure the time and distance a taxi travels. This information enables cab drivers to accurately charge their customers.

---

c. 3500 BCE   c. 2000 BCE ▼   1662 ▲   1804 ▼   1863 ▲   1871 ▼   1881 ▲   1885 ▼   1891 ▲   1908 ▼

MODEL OF TREVITHICK'S STEAM ENGINE

Steam locomotion
British engineer Richard Trevithick builds the first steam-powered railroad locomotive. The four-wheeled engine travels at a top speed of 5 mph (8 km/h) and can haul wagons weighing 10 tons.

PENNY FARTHING

MODEL OF A CHARIOT

War chariots
Horse-drawn chariots provide ancient civilizations, such as Egypt, Greece, and Mesopotamia, with speedy vehicles to use in battles held on flat, open ground.

Cycling craze
The Penny Farthing is invented and becomes a popular bicycle. The large front wheel measures around 59 in (1.5 m) in diameter, and enables riders to cross greater distances, while pedaling less.

DAIMLER'S MOTORCYCLE

Motorcycle
German inventor Gottlieb Daimler attaches a petroleum-powered four-stroke engine to a wooden bicycle and creates the world's first motorcycle.

HENRY FORD'S MODEL T

Ford's Model T
Henry Ford builds the Model T in Detroit, Michigan. Ford soon introduces a moving assembly line, dramatically cutting down labor costs. The Model T is widely considered to be the first affordable car.

Red to green

The first red-green automated electric traffic lights are developed by Lester Wire, a policeman from Salt Lake City, Utah. Yellow lights and buzzers are added later.

EARLY TRAFFIC LIGHTS

NAPIER-CAMPBELL'S BLUEBIRD

Land-speed record

Sir Malcolm Campbell's Napier-Campbell Bluebird is the first vehicle purpose-built to break the land-speed record, driving a record-breaking 281.44 kph (174.88 mph).

Skateboarding

Wooden skateboards are commercially produced for the first time in California. A skateboarding craze spreads across the USA and to other parts of the world.

EARLY WOODEN SKATEBOARD

Stunt bike

BMX (bicycle motocross) emerges in California. With small, 20-in (50.8-cm) knobbled tires, BMX bikes are originally built to race on sandy, hilly tracks. BMX freestyle, where riders perform tricks, develops from BMX racing.

BMX STUNT RIDER

THRUSTSSC

Sound barrier

British RAF pilot, Andy Green, drives the ThrustSSC to set a new land-speed record of 763.035 mph (1,227.99 km/h) in the Black Rock Desert, Nevada. The ThrustSSC is also the first land vehicle to break the sound barrier at Mach 1.

▲ 1912 1916 ▼ ▲ 1927 1958 ▼ ▲ 1960s 1964 ▼ ▲ 1970s 1994 ▼ ▲ 1997 2004 ▼

Armored tank

The army tank is invented by the British for use in World War I. The tank's heavy riveted metal armor protects the soldiers inside from weapon fire, and the unique flat "caterpillar tracks" can traverse muddy, uneven terrain.

BRITISH MARK V TANK

Super seller

The Honda Super Cub is introduced and goes on to become the world's best-selling motor vehicle, with sales exceeding 35 million bikes.

HONDA SUPER CUB

Bullet train

The world's first high-speed rail service begins with Japan's *Shinkansen* (bullet train). The first bullet train travels 332 miles (535 km) between Tokyo and Osaka in under four hours, reaching speeds of 124 mph (200 km/h).

JAPANESE BULLET TRAIN

Tunnel link

The Channel Tunnel between Britain and mainland Europe is completed, stretching 31 miles (50 km) and lying 131 ft (40 m) beneath the English Channel. It consists of three tunnels: two are for trains, while a third tunnel is for maintenance workers and emergency access.

CHANNEL TUNNEL TERMINAL

Hybrid car

The Toyota Prius is the world's first mass-produced, midsized hybrid car. The car switches between a gasoline-powered engine and an emission-free electric motor.

TOYOTA PRIUS

Traffic controls

Stop! Go! Yield! One way! Dead end! Around the world, signs and signals enforce traffic rules, and safely direct motor vehicles, cyclists, and pedestrians on the roads. The simple words, bright colors, and bold graphic symbols ensure that road users quickly understand what the instruction means.

Pedestrian crossing (the Netherlands)
This is called a "zebra crossing" in the USA and UK because of the stripes.

BUS ZONE
3.00 PM – 6.30 PM
MON–FRI →

NO STOPPING
←

LOADING ZONE
7.00 AM – 3.00 PM
MON–FRI
→

No parking zones (Australia)
This area is restricted to buses and vehicles loading goods.

Speed limit (France)
The speed limit on many urban roads is 18.6 mph (30 km/h).

Bike lane (Austria)
Only bicycles can travel in this designated lane.

Double lines (UK)
Yellow double lines indicate "no parking" zones.

No entry (France)
Traffic is not allowed to proceed any further.

Wild elk (Canada)
Animals such as wild elk can be a hazard on forest roads.

Melting snow (Canada)
Heavy snow melting from rooftops can be dangerous to passersby.

DETOUR

INTERSTATE **295** INTERSTATE **395**

SOUTH

7 ST NW
100

Signpost (USA)
Signposts can be crammed with traffic information.

Stop sign (Morocco)
Red octagons signal "stop" in many parts of the world.

Wild bears (Japan)
Forest visitors are warned that bears are in the vicinity.

熊出没
注意!!
佐井村・大間営林署・大間警察署

ATTENTION!

قف

7–9:30AM
4–6:30PM
MONDAY–FRIDAY

Directions post (Ireland)
Road users are given the distances to towns in all directions.

UACHTARÁRD
TOUGHTERARD
71 GAILLIMH
GALWAY 2

L SCRIOB
100 SCREEBE 5

Traffic lights (India)
Traffic lights glow red, yellow, and green to tell vehicles whether to stop, wait, or go.

Autorickshaw stand (India)
People can line up for an autorickshaw at this stand.

Street sign (Israel)
The name of this street is written in Hebrew, Arabic, and Latin.

ויאה דולורוזה

طريق الآلام

VIA DOLOROSA

No right turning

Camera: 10   Monitor: 50

Traffic control center (UK)
Masses of closed-circuit television (CCTV) screens in traffic control centers show engineers the status of traffic on the roads. With this information, engineers can detect accidents and monitor congestion.

No horns (Egypt)
Noise pollution can be a problem in big cities. This sign forbids the use of car horns.

ATH SALACH
ECESS 9½
OCHÁN T71
IFDEN 23

DROICHEAD MHAMA 5 L
MAAM BRIDGE   100
IONÁN
EENANE 13

Δράμα 36
Drama
Θεσσαλονίκη 161
Thesaloniki

Directions sign (Greece)
Highway users are informed of the distances to towns they are approaching.

Customs sign (Croatia)
A customs checkpoint is located at the border.

CARINA
DOUANE

鷹峯 Takagamine   宝ヶ池 Takaragaike
鞍馬 Kurama   修学院 Shugakuin
←40 北山通り 103→
国立京都国際会館 →
Kyoto International Conference Hall 2.5Km

Directions sign (Japan)
Directions are given to nearby towns, tourist attractions, and highways.

The passengers

For the passengers arriving and departing from Shivaji Stadium Terminal every day, buses are a cheap and convenient way of getting around the city. Some use the buses to commute to work or school, while others use them to go shopping or visit friends.

Vikas and Aakash

Brothers Vikas and Aakash make the hour-long journey to school by bus. "We enjoy the ride with our friends."

Raju

Vendor Raju sells plastic toy balls at the station. He carries his stock to and from home every day on a bus. "I have to pay an extra fare for my stock," he explains.

Pallavi

Relaxing after a shopping trip, Pallavi stops for a snack before catching a bus home. "I like riding the bus," she says. "I find them hassle-free."

Anil

Sculptor Anil is on his way to view some exhibitions. "I am an avid observer of people, and the buses in Delhi carry lots of good subjects for me."

Roshni

"The bus is cheaper than a taxi or auto-rickshaw," says Roshni, who is traveling to a hospital across the city for a check-up.

Sudhir

A regular bus user, Sudhir travels 9 miles (15 km) every day to a market near the terminal to buy flowers. "I carry them back on the bus to sell in my shop."

On board

"Munchie" vendors board buses at the depot and at busy stops to sell fruit and snacks to the passengers. Buses can get very crowded, especially during rush hours, when some passengers have to stand and hold on to an overhead bar.

Getting around

■ Delhi is one of India's largest cities, with a population of 13.8 million people.
■ Buses are the most popular form of public transportation in the city.
■ 1.98 million passengers travel on buses in Delhi every day and 72.6 million bus trips are made every year.
■ A Green Card—a day pass for all Delhi buses—costs 25 rupees (50 cents).
■ The bus system is often referred to by locals as *Daudo to Chado* ("Run to Climb") because of the very short stoppage times at bus stops.
■ There are 24,774 buses on the roads of Delhi, compared to 1.3 million cars, 2.7 million motorcycles and scooters, 74,906 auto-rickshaws, and 14,941 taxis.
■ Interstate bus services connect Delhi with other parts of North India, and a bus service operates between Delhi and Lahore, Pakistan.

The Indian capital, Delhi, is a big, bustling city. Many people rely on cars to get around, but for those without their own wheels, there is an extensive bus network to transport them around. Shivaji Stadium Terminal in central Delhi is a busy bus depot. Every day thousands of passengers arrive to and depart from the station, on their way to or returning from nearby stores and offices.

Shivaji Stadium
Bus Depot
Delhi

Snack stop
Stalls selling salty and sweet snacks are set up on sidewalks around the bus station.

The workers

Drivers, conductors, mechanics, and traffic inspectors work together to ensure the bus services run efficiently and on time. The state-run Delhi Transport Corporation (DTC) is the largest of the city's bus companies.

Sahab

"I get to talk to a lot of people on my route, so time passes really quickly," explains bus conductor Sahab.

Hansraj

"I make the garlands myself," says Hansraj. He sells flower garlands to bus drivers who put them on Hindu shrines in the front of their buses.

Inderjeet

Traffic inspector Inderjeet has been working for the DTC for 38 years. "When I started, the Shivaji hockey stadium hadn't even been built!"

S. A. Khan

"I start my shift at 6 a.m. and finish at 2:30 p.m.," says time keeper S. A. Kahn. He checks that buses arrive and depart on schedule.

Karamveer

"I get paid on a kilometer basis, so the more I work and the more I drive, the more I earn," says DTC bus driver Karamveer.

On the road

It is not just other vehicles that Delhi's bus drivers must look out for. Elephants and camels are sometimes ridden along the roads by their owners. Cows, which are sacred to the Hindu religion, can also roam the streets.

Bus business

■ The Delhi Transport Corporation (DTC) runs 3,200 buses from its own fleet and about 2,600 buses from private contractors.
■ The DTC network of buses has a total of 300 routes across the city.

■ Around 29,200 people are employed by the DTC, including drivers, conductors, traffic supervisors, repair and maintenance and administrative staff.
■ All buses, taxis, and auto-rickshaws must

have CNG (compressed natural gas) engines to help combat pollution in the city.
■ Buses, taxis, and auto-rickshaws older than 15 years are banned in Delhi.
■ A subway system is being constructed

in the city to help combat the chronic road congestion. The first underground lines opened in 2005.
■ The DTC operates bus routes to connect commuters with the new subway stations.

- 67 percent of urban roads are congested during rush hour.

- The phrase "rush hour" was first used in 1898.

- In 1960, 4 percent of the world's population owned a car.

- The time lost to traffic jams in a large city is the equivalent to seven people's entire working lives every day.

- The UK is Europe's most-congested country, with 10,000 jams a week.

- Today, 12 per cent of the world's population own a car.

- In the USA, people spend more than 100 hours a year commuting.

- New York City's traffic crawls at an average 6.2 mph (10 km/h).

- The highway around London is the busiest road in Europe.

- Drivers in Seattle are stuck in jams for about 60 hours a year.

- Weekday traffic speeds in Shanghai, China, are just 5.5 mph (9 km/h).

- In 45 BCE, Rome banned all vehicles from the city because of traffic jams.

- Almost 13 million cars were recycled in 1997—this would create a line of traffic circling Earth one and a quarter times.

- The European Union organizes an annual car-free day so that people can experience jam-free cities.

- The longest traffic jam ever was 109 miles (176 km) long, stretching from Lyon to Paris, France, on February 16, 1980.

- The highest traffic jam was at a pass in the Dangla Mountains in China, where more than 1,000 vehicles lined up in 2004.

- Signals from cellphones are used to work out traffic-jam hotspots in Finland.

Traffic jam

Have you ever been on a highway when the traffic starts to slow down? Bumper to bumper, a line of cars crawls along ahead of you. You're in a jam! There are more than 500 million motor vehicles in the world today, and, if present trends continue, the number of cars on Earth will double within 30 years; by which time, scientists predict, traffic congestion will become 10 times worse than it is today.

■ Jams cost a typical city $900 million in lost work time every year.

■ The average commuter spends 46 hours in jams.

■ In 1868, the first traffic lights controlled horse-drawn carriages and pedestrians in London.

■ In Athens, Greece, only cars with odd-numbered license plates can drive in the city on odd-numbered days, and vice versa for even-numbered cars.

■ On April 12, 1990, a record jam of 18 million cars was reported on the East-West German border as Soviet rule came to an end.

■ A hospital in Norway had to build a new road lane because people kissing loved ones goodbye were causing traffic jams.

■ Traffic police in parts of Asia wear face masks to protect themselves from traffic fumes.

■ In India, cows are a major cause of traffic jams. Considered sacred, they are free to wander onto roads.

■ UN-trained traffic police have controlled the daily jams in Monrovia, Liberia, since the city's traffic lights stopped working in 1990.

■ The longest traffic jam in Japanese history was 84 miles (135 km) long and involved 15,000 vehicles.

■ Traffic jams use up to 5.7 billion gallons (26 billion liters) of fuel each year. The world's oil reserves could run out in less than 100 years.

Car construction

The Gläserne Manufaktur ("transparent factory") in Dresden, Germany, handles the final assembly of the Volkswagen Phaeton car. The factory was specially designed to make car construction visible to visitors and people living nearby. It has walls made entirely of glass and oval-shaped floors with embedded conveyor belts. Most of the work is performed by hand, by highly skilled factory workers. Robots are only used to transport parts around the factory and undertake heavy, arduous tasks. Customers can visit the factory and get involved in every stage of the construction of their own custom-made car, from selecting the color and the interior finish, to watching the parts being fitted.

1 Preassembled components are delivered to a warehouse on the outskirts of the city. They are taken as needed to the factory on a specially developed tram, the "CarGoTram."

2 Parts for each car are stacked onto carts. It takes eight cartloads to make each car. Once loaded, the carts are taken by robot to the factory floor.

3 A car's suspension and drivetrain (all the parts that power the car, including the engine) are worked on separately from the body of the car.

4 A slow-moving conveyor belt built into the floor carries the car bodies around the factory. Workers are responsible for different tasks, such as wiring lights and installing seats.

5 The drivetrain is connected with the car body in a process called the "marriage." The entire procedure, including bolt-fastening, is automated.

6 Robots are used for any heavy work. One robot installs the storage for the spare tire, another the wheels on the car, and a third the front and rear windshields.

7 When constuction is finished the car is thoroughly checked and tested. Visual checks of the paint finish and body panels are conducted in large light booths.

Delivery time

After their sales documents are processed, customers can look at the information boards to check on the progress of their car delivery and find out which bay they need to go to for pickup.

Tower storage

Cars to be delivered that day are brought on an automated conveyor belt from the factory to the car tower. A central elevator carries the cars up the tower to a bay allocated by the tower's computer system.

Car lift

The computer system is programmed with a schedule of the day's deliveries. It instructs one of the two elevators to rise up to the correct bay in the tower. A robotic arm slides out from the elevator and reaches under the car, raising it slightly so it can be conveyed onto the elevator. Once loaded, the elevator descends to the drive-out level.

Car
tower

Instead of picking up their new vehicles from a car dealer, Volkswagen customers in Europe can travel to the Autostadt, an automobile-inspired theme park in Wolfsburg, Germany. While car owners wander around the pavilions, their brand-new cars travel by conveyor belt from the nearby factory to be stored in two fully automated 160-ft- (48-m-) high glass towers. When it is time for a car to be delivered to its new owner, a huge mechanical elevator swings into action, locates the bay the car is held in, and lowers it to the ground, where another conveyor belt takes it to the delivery bay.

AUTOTÜRME

The cylindrical AutoTürme (car tower) combines the technologies of three classic inventions—the multistory parking lot, the forklift, and the elevator—to create a unique high-rise stacking system. A central mechanism in the tower operates two elevators, which convey vehicles to and from the 400 car bays.

Specifications:	
Height	160 ft (48 m)
Number of storeys	20
Number of car bays	400
Despatch frequency	Every 45 seconds
Lift speed	4.5 mph (7 km/h)
Lift rotation	270 degrees
Time it takes to reach distribution centre from tower	4 minutes

Belt to bay
From the tower, the cars are taken on robotic pallets along a conveyor belt to one of four bays. When the car arrives in a bay, the doors open and a member of staff drives the car to the fine finish area.

Fine finish
The final checks of the car take place in the fine finish area. There can be as many as 280 different points to check, including the paintwork and interior finish. The license plate is attached and the car is ready.

Customer collection
The customer is handed the keys to the car and can drive away.

Super speed

Campbell Bluebird
Sir Malcolm Campbell broke several land-speed records in the 1920s and 1930s driving his Bluebird vehicles. On September 3, 1935, he recorded his fastest and final record.

Top speed:
301.129 mph
(484.620 km/h)

Railton Mobil Special
On September 16, 1947, John R. Cobb raced across the Bonneville Salt Flats in the Railton Mobil Special. This record was held for an incredible 16 years.

Top speed:
394.19 mph
(634.39 km/h)

Blue Flame
In the rocket-powered Blue Flame, Gary Gabelich claimed the land-speed record on October 23, 1970. The machine's name was inspired by its fuel—natural liquid gas.

Top speed:
630.389 mph
(1,014.52 km/h)

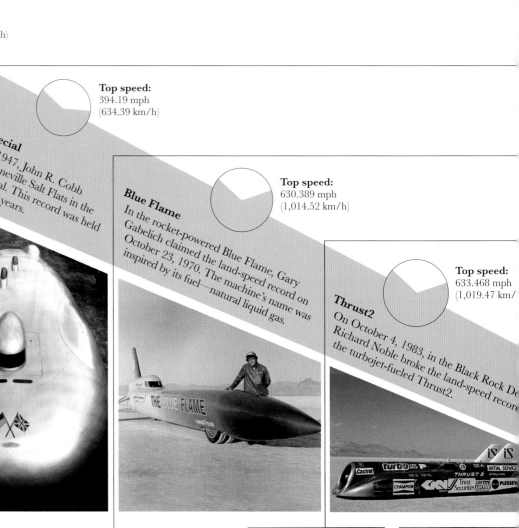

Thrust2
On October 4, 1983, in the Black Rock De Richard Noble broke the land-speed recore the turbojet-fueled Thrust2.

Top speed:
633.468 mph
(1,019.47 km/

Since automobiles were invented, people have pushed them to go faster. Rocketing through the desert at mind-boggling speeds, a vehicle making a land-speed record attempt is a sight to behold. Dashing into the record books, land-speed record drivers risk life and limb on their brief and volatile journeys. Fired with jet or rocket-engine thrust, land-speed record vehicles look more like spaceships dreamed up in science fiction films than cars.

Top speed:
763.035 mph
(1,227.99 km/h)

ThrustSSC (SuperSonic Car)

On October 15, 1997, fired on two Rolls-Royce Spey jet engines, the ThrustSSC was the first land vehicle to officially break the sound barrier at Mach 1. Driven by Andy Green of Britain, the ThrustSSC set a new land-speed record of 763.035 mph (1,227.99 km/h) in the Black Rock Desert in the US. The open, flat surface of the unpopulated desert provides the perfect environment for land-speed attempts.

Classic cars

From luxury sports cars to family sedans, some vehicles go down in history for their stellar performance and fine styling. Car enthusiasts will pay a small fortune to purchase their favorite classic car, and will go to great lengths to restore it with reconditioned parts and maintain its original color and form. While some classics such as the AC 428 were limited editions with very few cars produced, the Mustang "pony car" was the fastest-selling Ford ever, with more than two million of them sold between 1964 and 1970.

Pontiac Chieftain, 1949
0–60 mph (0–96 km/h): 13 seconds
Number produced: N/A
Country of origin: US

Land Rover Series 1, 1949
0–60 mph (0–96 km/h): N/A
Number produced: 3,000
Country of origin: UK

Bentley R-Type Continental, 1952–55
0–60 mph (0–96 km/h): 13.5 seconds
Number produced: 208
Country of origin: UK

Lancia Aurelia, 1954–56
0–60 mph (0–96 km/h): 14.3 seconds
Number produced: 330
Country of origin: Italy

Mercedes 300SL Gullwing, 1954–57
0–60 mph (0–96 km/h): 8.8 seconds
Number produced: 1,400
Country of origin: Germany

AC Ace Bristol, 1956–61
0–60 mph (0–96 km/h): 9.1 seconds
Number produced: 463
Country of origin: UK

Chrysler New Yorker, 1957
0–60 mph (0–96 km/h): 12.3 seconds
Number produced: 34,620
Country of origin: US

Lotus Elite, 1957–63
0–60 mph (0–96 km/h): 11.1 seconds
Number produced: 988
Country of origin: UK

Buick Limited Series 700 Rivera, 1958
0–60 mph (0–96 km/h): 9.5 seconds
Number produced: 7,436
Country of origin: US

Austin Healey Sprite Mk1, 1958–61
0–60 mph (0–96 km/h): 20.5 seconds
Number produced: 38,999
Country of origin: UK

Ford Fairlane 500 Skyliner, 1959
0–60 mph (0–96 km/h): 10.6 seconds
Number produced: 12,915
Country of origin: US

Ferrari 250 GT SWB, 1959–62
0–60 mph (0–96 km/h): 6.6 seconds
Number produced: 167
Country of origin: Italy

Porsche 356B, 1959–63
0–60 mph (0–96 km/h): 10 seconds
Number produced: 30,963
Country of origin: Germany

Daimler SP250 Dart, 1959–64
0–60 mph (0–96 km/h): 8.5 seconds
Number produced: 2,644
Country of origin: UK

NSU Sport Prinz, 1959–67
0–60 mph (0–96 km/h): 27.7 seconds
Number produced: 20,831
Country of origin: Germany

Citroën DS Décapotable, 1960–71
0–60 mph (0–96 km/h): 11.2 seconds
Number produced: 1,365
Country of origin: France

Jaguar E-type, 1961–74
0–60 mph (0–96 km/h): 7.2 seconds
Number produced: 72,520
Country of origin: UK

Rolls-Royce Silver Cloud, 1962–65
0–60 mph (0–96 km/h): 10.8 seconds
Number produced: 2,044
Country of origin: UK

MGB, 1962–80
0–60 mph (0–96 km/h): 12.2 seconds
Number produced: 512,000
Country of origin: UK

Skoda Felicia, 1963
0–60 mph (0–96 km/h): 27.5 seconds
Number produced: 15,864
Country of origin: Czech Republic

Chevrolet Corvette Stingray, 1963–67
0–60 mph (0–96 km/h): 5.4 seconds
Number produced: 118,964
Country of origin: US

Renault Alpine A110, 1963–77
0–60 mph (0–96 km/h): 8.7 seconds
Number produced: 8,203
Country of origin: France

Lincoln Continental, 1964
0–60 mph (0–96 km/h): 11 seconds
Number produced: 3,328
Country of origin: USA

Gordon Keeble GT, 1964–67
0–60 mph (0–96 km/h): 7.5 seconds
Number produced: 104
Country of origin: UK

Ford Mustang, 1964–70
0–60 mph (0–96 km/h): 6.1 seconds
Number produced: 2,077,826
Country of origin: USA

Datsun Fairlady, 1965–70
0–60 mph (0–96 km/h): 13.3 seconds
Number produced: 40,000
Country of origin: Japan

Lamborghini Miura, 1966–72
0–60 mph (0–96 km/h): 6.7 seconds
Number produced: 800
Country of origin: Italy

AC 428, 1966–73
0–60 mph (0–96 km/h): 5.9 seconds
Number produced: 80
Country of origin: UK

Jensen Interceptor, 1966–76
0–60 mph (0–96 km/h): 7.3 seconds
Number produced: 1,500
Country of origin: UK

Maserati Ghibli, 1967
0–60 mph (0–96 km/h): 6.2 seconds
Number produced: 1,274
Country of origin: Italy

Chevrolet Camaro RS, 1967–70
0–60 mph (0–96 km/h): 8.3 seconds
Number produced: 231,581
Country of origin: USA

Saab Sonett V4, 1968
0–60 mph (0–96 km/h): 12 seconds
Number produced: 10,249
Country of origin: Sweden

Mercedes 280SL, 1968–71
0–60 mph (0–96 km/h): 9.3 seconds
Number produced: 23,885
Country of origin: Germany

Alfa Romeo Spider, 1968–78
0–60 mph (0–96 km/h): 11.2 seconds
Number produced: 7,237
Country of origin: Italy

Triumph TR6, 1969–76
0–60 mph (0–96 km/h): 29 seconds
Number produced: 94,619
Country of origin: UK

Porsche 911 Carrera RS, 1972–73
0–60 mph (0–96 km/h): 5.6 seconds
Number produced: 1,580
Country of origin: Germany

Aston Martin V8, 1972–89
0–60 mph (0–96 km/h): 6.2 seconds
Number produced: 2,842
Country of origin: UK

Peugeot 504, 1974
0–60 mph (0–96 km/h): 11 seconds
Number produced: 977
Country of origin: France

Cadillac Seville, 1978
0–60 mph (0–96 km/h): 11.5 seconds
Number produced: 56,985
Country of origin: USA

BMW M1, 1978–80
0–60 mph (0–96 km/h): 5.4 seconds
Number produced: 457
Country of origin: Germany

Mazda RX7, 1978–85
0–60 mph (0–96 km/h): 8.9 seconds
Number produced: 474,565
Country of origin: Japan

Delorean DMC12, 1979–82
0–60 mph (0–96 km/h): 9.6 seconds
Number produced: 6,500
Country of origin: UK

Audi Quattro Sport, 1983–87
0–60 mph (0–96 km/h): 4.8 seconds
Number produced: 80
Country of origin: Germany

Lancia Delta HF Integrale, 1986–92
0–60 mph (0–96 km/h): 6.6 seconds
Number produced: N/A
Country of origin: Italy

Chevrolet Corvette ZR1, 1996
0–60 mph (0–96 km/h): 3.9 seconds
Number produced: N/A
Country of origin: USA

Morgan Roadster V6, 2004–
0–60 mph (0–96 km/h): 4.9 seconds
Number produced: N/A
Country of origin: UK

Exhaust manifold

Fan belt

Bell housing

Rear muffler

Ignition key

Oil filter

Oil sump

Reflectors

Handmade aluminum hood

Front hood

Five-leaf rear spring

Hand brake

Support beam

Track rod

Joint

Rear axle

Decorative edging

Wooden chassis

Coolant pipes

Alternator

Clutch pressure pad

Differential housing

Body paint

Wheel spoke

Steering wheel

Hole for fuel filler cap

Aluminum back panel

Carpet

Windshield-wiper motor

Grill hinges

Bracket

Arm

Blade

Nut

Headlight

Front radiator cowl

Hole for headlight

Front fender

Constructing the car

The Morgan Roadster has a wooden body frame. It is carved from ash—a strong, durable, and lightweight wood. The frame is covered with aluminum panels, which are carefully cut to ensure a perfect fit. Next, the engine, gearbox, and suspension are assembled to the chassis, or frame. The dashboard, windshield, sidescreens, exhaust, lights, and gasoline caps are fitted, and the handmade leather seats and hood are installed. Customers can decide what color they want the interior of their Morgan to be. The body of the car is sanded and painted—again to the customer's specifications. Before being delivered to customers, the cars are checked against a quality list, then washed and polished.

Bolt hole

Hub cap

Connector

Front signal lights

Rear signal lights

Light connector

Angled rod

Aerial

Glove compartment door

Holes for gauges

Walnut dashboard

Hole for rev counter

Rocker covers

Coolant outlet

Oil filler cap

Oil dipstick

Engine block

Fuel cable

Hole for speedometer

Engine lifting eye

Water reservoir

Morgan logo ornament

Sliding sidescreen window

Left-hand sidescreen

Wiring harness

Welded joint

Muffler

Connectors

Coolant temperature

Aluminum panel

Door mirror

Mirror edging

Hinged joint

Vents

Bolt hole

"Waterfall" radiator grill

Door handle

Fuel gauge

Tachometer

Clamp

Suspension springs

Aluminum rear fender

Aerial bracket

Air intake vents

MORGAN

Modern legend

The majority of cars built today are designed by computers and constructed on fully automated assembly lines. But some luxury cars, such as this Morgan Roadster, are hand-built using traditional skills. The flowing lines and nostalgic look of the Morgan make it very popular, and customers have to join a waiting list of up to one year before they can own one. When it gets to

their turn, however, they can hand-pick the color and all the hardware and fittings of their custom-built sportscar. The Morgan factory in England builds just 600 cars per year, and the average production time for one Morgan sportscar is 23 days.

Room for two
Like all sportscars, the compact Morgan Roadster can only carry two people—the driver and one passenger. The seats are covered in leather, and the dashboard is carved from wood.

Engine power

Although the Morgan Roadster looks like a car from decades past, it contains a powerful and lightweight modern engine and can reach a top speed of 134 mph (215 km/h).

At the back

A spare tire is attached to the rear of the car in case of a flat tire. Also stored at the back of the car is a folded roof, which can be pulled over for protection when it rains.

Red lens

Leather upholstery

Brake caliper servo

Brake bracket

Brake clamp

Connector

Worm gear

Brake cylinder

Brake

Driver's seat

Passenger's seat

Seat belt catches

Connecting cable

Side lights

Door lock keys

Door handle

Bolt hole

Reflector bracket

Bolt hole

Galvanized chassis

Aluminum rear wing

Flywheels

Fuel cap

Aluminum molding

Mirror edging

Thread

Shock absorber

Drive shaft

Drive shaft bracket

Side mirror

Suspension weight

Winkers

Rearview mirror

Windshield

Nuts

Bolts

Speedometer

Aerial bracket and spindle

Brackets

Oil pressure gauge

Door handle

Right-hand sidescreen

Battery gauge

Sidescreen brackets

Air intake vents

Side louvers

Front hood

Battery

Crown wheel

Electric cable

Propeller shaft

Stainless steel wheel

Connecting cable

Brake lights

Strengthened edging

Tire

Gearstick head

Logo

Alloy clamp

Wheel nut

Fan blade

Fan

Spoke

Tread

Clamp

Exhaust

Front fender

Rack-and-pinion steering mechanism

Axle

Worm gear

Support strut

Groove

Windshield wipers

Hole for headlight

Vulcanized rubber

Green car

Cars have transformed people's lives, freeing them to travel whenever and wherever they want. Unfortunately, cars also pollute the atmosphere. They pump out poisons and carbon dioxide—a gas that contributes to global warming. Another problem is that cars consume gasoline and diesel, and these expensive resources will eventually run out. Public transportation is not always the answer because services in rural areas are often infrequent. The compromise is to design cars with little or no impact on the environment. Solutions include minimizing the fuel that cars guzzle and using alternative types of power.

Going green

■ Bioethanol (an alcohol derived from plant sugars) produces 65 percent less greenhouse gases than gasoline.

■ Firefighters must undergo special training in order to manage the high voltages involved in electric and gasoline-electric car accidents.

■ In London, electric cars do not pay the city's congestion charge. Similarly, green cars in Norway can use the less crowded bus lanes.

Urban runaround
Designed in the USA, manufactured in India, and launched in the UK in 2004, the Reva G-Wiz is an electric car designed for urban use. About as long as a conventional car is wide, the Reva G-Wiz is extremely compact and easy to park in crowded city streets. Many countries offer drivers incentives for choosing to go green. Since it is officially classed as a quadracycle (four-wheeled bicycle) rather than a car, Reva G-Wiz drivers do not have to pay road tax in the UK.

The rear seats fold flat to give extra storage.

The high seats provide superior visibility.

Lightweight steering

Additional storage

Connection point to charge up batteries.

Eight batteries power the vehicle.

Interior view

The Reva G-Wiz's power pack has eight 6V lead acid batteries that power the car's 17.5 hp motor. Their weight also gives the car stability when turning. An onboard charger converts mains power into battery power. Computers control the flow of electricity between the charger, power pack, and motor.

Dashboard displays

The Reva G-Wiz has a touch-screen computer behind the steering wheel. It displays the speedometer, level of battery charge, and distance traveled. It also contains the satellite navigation system and controls the built-in MP3 player.

Charging up

With a top speed of 40 mph (65 km/h), the Reva G-Wiz can travel 40 miles (65 km) before its batteries run out. The battery is charged by being plugged into a mains supply. The car has a 16.5-ft- (5-m) long lead that connects into a standard 13 amp socket. It takes six hours to fully recharge the battery.

Energy-saving cars

Alternative fuels for internal combustion engines include compressed natural gas (CNG), liquefied petroleum gas (LPG), and biofuels such as bioethanol. Brazil and Sweden both have state-run biofuel programs, and in Brazil biofuel cars outsell ordinary ones. Alternative fuels are cleaner than gasoline or diesel, but none produce zero emissions (no harmful pollutants at all). Electric cars do, but their power is limited to minimal speeds and very short distances. Hybrid cars have a battery and an engine, so they get the best of both worlds.

Power mix

The popular, hybrid Toyota Prius uses electricity for speeds up to 30 mph (48 km/h)—the usual speed limit in cities. It generates this itself by recovering the waste energy lost as the car brakes. When traveling at higher speeds, the car switches to a .4-gallon (1.5-liter) gasoline engine.

Running on sunlight

Designed by Japanese students, the Luciole has solar cells on its roof and trunk that convert sunlight energy into electrical power. Just 4 ft (1.2 m) wide, the Luciole has only one front and one rear seat. It can reach speeds of 93 mph (150 kph), but will not move at all without sunlight.

Electric bubble

The Nissan Pivo concept car was showcased in 2005. Its bubble-shaped cabin turns full circle, so the car does not need a reverse gear. The car has good environmental credentials as no pollutants are produced by its lithium ion battery and electric motor.

People's car

In the 1930s, the German car engineer Ferdinand Porsche began work on a car that would revolutionize private transportation. His goal was to produce a reliable, affordable vehicle that could carry a family of five at a speed of 60 mph (100 km/h). Aside from its unique air-cooled rear engine, the resulting Volkswagen (German for "people's car") Type 1's most noticeable feature was its rounded, insectlike shape, which led to its nickname— "the Beetle." The Type 1 VW Beetle became one of the world's most popular cars. In its 65-year history, more than 21 million classic Beetles were produced.

Beetle mania

■ The Beetle was not the only cult Volkswagen vehicle. Introduced in 1950, the VW Type 2 (better known as the camper van) was a hit with hippies.

■ In 1938, the classic Beetle's engine volume was 60 cu in (985 cc). By 2003, its capacity had grown to 98 cu in (1.6 liters).

■ Most car engines are water-cooled. The Beetle's highly effective air cooling system had a surprise side effect: it gave the car its own distinctive sound!

■ The last original Beetle left the Volkswagen factory in Puebla, Mexico, on July 30, 2003. It is now in the Autostadt Museum, Wolfsburg.

1. The radiator contains water that helps to moderate the temperature of the engine.

2. Electrically operated, the fan is an additional method of cooling the car's engine.

3. The engine drives the wheels via the gearbox. Certain speeds relate to different gear ratios.

4. The body of the car is attached to connected steel tubes, which include the chassis rail.

5. Pedals are levers operated by the driver's feet to control the speed of the car.

6. A steering column shaft joins the steering wheel and the rack to which the wheels are attached.

7. The transmission tunnel is a metal container through which the gear lever connects the gearbox.

8. A driver-operated gearstick lever changes the gear according to the speed required.

9. The airbag housing contains an airbag used to reduce passengers' injuries in the event of a collision. The airbag is filled with gas that travels up the steering column.

10. The strong support legs that hold the roof of the car on to the rest of the body are called pillars.

11. The sunroof "window" in the car's roof can be opened to allow in extra light and fresh air.

12. An adjustable seat frame allows the driver or passenger to adjust the position and height of the seat.

13. The rear-door speaker transmits in-car entertainment to passengers sitting in the rear of the car.

14. The strong strap of the inertia reel seatbelt holds passengers in their seats in the event of a collision.

15. Electrically operated wires in the rear windshield heat up the glass to defrost ice and prevent misting.

16. The headrest unit is designed to protect occupants' heads in the event of a high-speed impact.

17. The muffler reduces the sound made by the Beetle's engine exhaust pipe.

18. Above the muffler in the rear of the car, the trunk floor offers an area to store luggage.

19. The rear bumper has been designed to cushion impact in the event of a collision.

In 1955, the one-millionth Volkswagen car, a gold-colored Beetle, was produced in the company's factory in Wolfsburg, Germany.

Herbie, who first gained popularity in the 1968 Disney film *The Love Bug*, is a Beetle with a mind of its own and the ability to drive itself.

At Beetle festivals, such as Bug Jam in the UK, enthusiasts exhibit their cars, swap parts, and participate in drag races, Beetle against Beetle!

Volkswagen launched the New Beetle in 1998. Unlike the original Beetle, the New Beetle's engine is at the front instead of the rear.

On the road

When people load up their car and take a road trip, the excitement is not always in the destination, but in the journey itself. While airplanes make long-distance travel swift and convenient, for many, an open road provides a sense of freedom and adventure. In reality, the road trip is often zigzagged with congested highways that have been mapped and signposted long ago. Some road trips are famous, with travelers reveling in the nostalgia of the former Route 66 in the United States, and the spectacular rugged southern coastline of Australia's Great Ocean Road, to enjoying the epic adventure of driving from Alaska to Chile on the Pan-American Highway.

Circle, Alaska
13,769 miles
(22,160 km)

Puerto Montt,
Chile
2,262 miles
(3,640 km)

Pan-American Highway,
Alaska to Chile

Traversing 16,000 miles (25,800 km) along the American continent, the Pan-American Highway is a true intercontinental road trip, crossing 13 national borders. From Circle in Alaska's freezing north to balmy Puerto Montt down south in Chile, roadtrippers braving the astonishing length of the highway must pack for every climate and terrain imaginable.

Dempster Highway, Canada

Length 460 miles (741 km)

From Dawson City to Inuvik, the Dempster Highway crosses rugged Canadian wilderness to the Arctic Circle. Passing mountain ranges, canyons, and waterfalls, the aurora borealis (Northern Lights) can be seen on the highway from February to April.

Grand Trunk Road, India to Afghanistan

Length 1,615 miles (2,600 km)

Starting in Kolkata, India, crossing to Lahore, Pakistan, and ending in Kabul, Afghanistan, the 1,615-mile (2,600-km) Grand Trunk Road is historically known as "The Long Walk." With daredevil drivers, potholes, and roaming livestock, the Grand Trunk Road is a journey for the adventurous. .

Great Ocean Road, Australia

Length 150 miles (241 km)

Skimming steep cliffs along Australia's southern coastline, the Great Ocean Road stretches from surf town Torquay in Victoria to Nelson near the South Australian border. The road winds past giant limestone stacks called the 12 Apostles, historical shipwrecks, and rain forests in the Otway Ranges.

Karakoram Highway, Pakistan to China

Length 807 miles (1,300 km)

Bridging Kashgar in China to Havelian in Pakistan, the Karakoram Highway was completed in 1978 in very hostile terrain. Passing the Karakoram, Pamir, and Himalayan mountain ranges, plus glaciers, green valleys, and desert, the highway carries travelers, tradespeople, yaks, and bactrian camels.

The Silk Road, southern Asia

Length 5,000 miles (8,046 km)

With numerous interconnecting routes across southern Asia, the Silk Road was pivotal in the expansion of ancient civilizations in China, Egypt, India, and Rome. Spreading culture and international commerce, the Silk Road ceased functioning as a trade route in 1400.

Historical Route 66

Decommissioned as a highway in 1985, Route 66 is now a historical route, crossing from Chicago, Illinois, to Santa Monica, California. During the 1930s, poor farming families from the Midwest traveled Route 66 hoping for better lives and job opportunities on the wealthier west coast.

Chicago
1,182 miles
(1,902 km)

Santa Monica
612 miles
(985 km)

Taxi!

Cabs conveniently transport passengers directly to their chosen location. They can be hailed in the street, lined up for at a taxi stand, or ordered by telephoning a dispatch center. Taxis are often identified by their color or livery, such as the famous yellow cabs in New York City, black cabs in London, and red cabs in urban Hong Kong. For people flagging a cab, a light on a taxi's roof indicates whether it is vacant or occupied.

Dodging Delhi's jams

More vehicles cram Delhi's streets than any other city in India. Visitors to Delhi tend to use taxis, while locals prefer to take less expensive auto-rickshaws to get around. Taxis in Delhi are usually taken from a taxi stand or reserved via telephone, instead of being hailed in the street.

Cruising the Big Apple

In 1915, taxi fleet owner John D. Hertz formed the "Yellow Cab Company" after discovering that yellow is the most visible color from a distance. Today, more than 12,000 yellow cabs (known as "medallion taxis") roam the streets of New York City. With fewer than half of New Yorkers owning a car, it is estimated that more than 240 million passengers ride taxis across the city's five boroughs each year.

From Mayfair to Whitechapel

At the beginning of the 17th century, horse-drawn "hackney carriages" began providing taxi services in London. To drive one of London's famed black cabs today, potential drivers must pass a rigorous test called "The Knowledge." Applicants must memorize 320 routes and 25,000 streets within a 6-mile (9.6-km) radius of Charing Cross in the heart of London.

Tools of the trade

The taximeter, which was invented in 1891, enabled cab drivers to charge passengers for the exact distance traveled. Other taxi innovations were radio dispatch in the 1940s, and computerized dispatch in the 1980s. Increasingly, modern cabs are fitted with GPS (Global Positioning Systems). Using satellites to find the quickest routes for drivers, GPS technology (below) also assists cab companies in keeping better track of their fleets.

Cuban classics

Many of the cars in Cuba predate 1960, and have been sustained with spare parts or been mixed and matched to form hybrid cars. Classic 1950s American cars (such as Chevrolets and Oldsmobiles) cruise the main streets as *ruteros*—taxis running fixed routes. These taxis are often modified with extra seats welded to the car frame, creating room for at least eight passengers.

Taxi trivia

■ "Taxi" comes from the "taximeter," which measures the distance a cab travels. The word "cab" comes from "cabriolet," the name of 19th-century horse-drawn carriages used in Paris.

■ In 1636, the first taxi stand was established on the Strand in London. At that time, only 50 London carriages were permitted taxi licenses.

■ In 1914, during World War I, 6,000 French troops were transported to the First Battle of the Marne via taxicabs.

■ Drivers of black cabs in London are renowned for having a particularly large hippocampus, which is a section of the brain related to learning and forming memories.

■ The first known female taxi driver drove a New York cab in 1925. In 2005, 407 of New York's 40,000 taxi drivers were women.

Intrepid Thai tuk-tuks

Small but speedy three-wheeled tuk-tuks weave through the city streets. They are fitted with tiny two-stroke engines and have handlebar steering. Passengers cram into the back seat behind the driver's cabin. Tuk-tuks are not fitted with meters, so passengers must bargain with the driver for their fare first.

Japanese silver service

Immaculately maintained, cabs in Japan are driven by drivers wearing white gloves. Fitted with GPS, Japanese cabs are technologically advanced. Drivers operate the rear left door via a button on their dashboard to let passengers in and out. This also prevents fingerprints marking the door!

Going by cable

San Francisco in California has the world's oldest cable car system. Cable cars are a type of light railroad where the cars grip a moving cable.

Ups and downs

The first escalator was built in 1897 as a fairground attraction. They now feature in shopping centers and public buildings all around the world.

Urban movers

Moving many people quickly over short distances can present more of a challenge than long-distance travel. Town and city planners need efficient ways to move thousands of people from one place to another. The biggest crowds build up between transportation hubs such as air, rail, and bus terminals.

When town and city planners are successful, people move in a steady flow—even during the peak times of the rush hour. Solutions for city travel have to be clean and sustainable, so they do not contribute to urban pollution. Above all, they need to be as safe as possible for the users.

Rapid movement

In 2002, the Paris Metro unveiled the first *trottoir roulant rapide* (rapid-moving walkway). It carries around 110,000 pedestrians across busy Montparnasse station each day—a distance of 607 ft (185 m). Originally set at 7 mph (11 kph), the speed had to be lowered to 6 mph (9 kph) because so many passengers were falling down!

Traveling light

Trams are light railroads. In the 1950s, many cities phased out trams in favor of buses. Now, new tram systems are being constructed, including the system built for the 2004 Olympics in Athens, Greece. Unlike buses, trams do not produce exhaust fumes, and their routes often bypass other road traffic.

Single track

As its name suggests, a monorail is a railroad that has a single track. Compared to conventional railroads, which run on two parallel rails, a monorail takes up less space. It is an attractive solution for elevated rail routes because it blocks out less sky. The monorail is also able to turn, climb, and descend faster than two-track railroads.

Leaps and bounds

Not all urban travel is about finding a sensible route to work or school. Free-running (*le parkour*) began in the suburbs of Paris in the 1990s. It is an extreme sport that treats the city like an outsize obstacle course. Participants leap over rooftops and between buildings as smoothly and athletically as they can. It is a very dangerous activity, but the fluid movements can be exciting to watch.

The commuters

More than 2.5 million people travel on the Underground every day, crossing from one area of London to another. The Tube is a popular form of travel for Londoners, as well as the millions of tourists who visit the city every year.

Tatiana
Traveling on the Underground is convenient, according to Tatiana. "People are always happy to help me lift the buggy up and down stairs."

Jasper and Oliver
"We're taking the Tube to Heathrow Airport to go on vacation. The Tube is the fastest way to get around London."

Robin
"I travel to different Tube stations regularly to oversee the maintenance of the elevators and escalators. The Tube quick, clean, and very convenient."

Charlotta
"Traveling on the Tube is a great time to read or do a crossword puzzle," says Charlotta. "If I've forgotten a book, I love to people-watch."

Ben and Becky
"It is easy to visit London's famous landmarks on the Underground. We've just been to the Harrods department store to look at puppies."

Yumi
"The Underground is reliable and safe, and makes exploring London easy," says Yumi. From South Korea, she is on her way to college, where she studies English.

Rush hour
The busiest time on the Underground is when people are traveling to and from work in the morning and evening. Trains run more frequently during these rush-hour periods.

Getting around

- There are 275 Tube stations in London; 63 of them are in the central London area.
- The Underground has 12 different lines. They are represented by different colors on network maps.
- There are 976 million passenger trips each year—an average of 2.67 million a day.
- About 150,000 people enter London Underground stations every hour. The busiest station is Waterloo, which moves 46,000 people during the three-hour peak time in the morning—that is 255 people every minute.
- Every year, 77.5 million passengers pass through Kings Cross St. Pancras station.
- The circular logo to represent the Tube, called the roundel, first appeared in 1913.
- To help travelers get around, the Tube map was designed in 1933 by Harry Beck. He was inspired by the shape of electrical circuits and his design is still the basis of today's map.

London Underground

Beneath the streets of London lies a vast network of train tunnels and stations. London Underground is the oldest subway system in the world, and one of the largest, with 253 miles (408 km) of track. Despite its name, it runs both underground and overland and is nicknamed "the Tube" by Londoners.

Steel and glass
One of the newest stations in the east of the city, Canary Wharf's modern architecture has won awards.

The workers

To keep such a busy transportion system running efficiently, London Underground employs more than 12,500 people. Each person has a particular job to do, from driving trains and supervising platforms to handling emergencies.

David

"The Emergency Response Unit deals with everything from signal failure to cutting trees on overland sections," explains manager David.

Ted

"People leave the strangest things on the Underground, and they can cause security alerts," says Ted, who works in the huge lost property department.

Julian

"Meeting lots of people is the best thing about my job," says Julian, a customer services assistant. "And there is a great team spirit among the staff."

Said

"As duty station manager I run three stations and oversee 160 staff," says Said. "The Underground keeps London running."

Sue

"My job includes watching the platforms via CCTV cameras and making announcements to keep people safe and informed," Sue explains. "I like being in control!"

Anthony

"As a train driver on the Northern line, I work in shifts of two to three hours, although sometimes I'll work longer. I have now worked for London Underground for 34 years!"

Tube trivia

- Each Underground train travels a total distance of 73,500 miles (118,287 km) every year.
- The average Underground train speed is 20 mph (33 km/h).

- Today, the Underground is an electric railroad. However, when the first trains ran on the system they were powered by steam.
- Of the network's 253 miles (408 km) of track, 45 percent is underground.

- Many Tube stations were used as air-raid shelters during World War II.
- 410 escalators and 102 elevators transport passengers from surface to platform throughout the system.

- Hampstead station is the deepest station below street level, lying 192 ft (58.5 m) underground.
- The Underground is closed for five hours every night so that repairs can be made.

Going underground

Mazes of tunnels run beneath about 100 major cities of the world, with trains seamlessly transporting masses of commuters from place to place. Known variously as the subway, the metro, the Underground, or the Tube, underground railroads are highly effective rapid-transit systems. Bypassing traffic jams and congestion in the streets above, these hidden public transportation networks keep big cities on the move. Even at night, when most rail systems are shut, teams of engineers carry out maintenance work and safety checks to keep the rails running smoothly.

London
In 1863, the world's first underground railroad opened in the United Kingdom, revolutionizing public transportation. The Underground was steam-powered until the Northern Line introduced electric traction in 1890, making for a cleaner ride. With 12 busy lines, the Underground network now runs over 258 miles (415 km).

New York City
In the United States, the IRT (Interborough Rapid Transit) subway network opened in 1904 to ease the city's traffic problems. The 24-hour subway now has 277 of its 468 stations situated underground. Running every four minutes in rush hour, the subway shuttles an estimated 4.7 million passengers around New York City each workday.

○ **Mexico City**   ○ **Toronto**   ○ **Buenos Aires**   ○ **Glasgow**   ○ **Oslo**   ○ **Berlin**   ○ **Budapest**

Mexico City's metro is the world's cheapest, with a one-way fare costing two *pesos* (18¢). During the metro's construction, ancient Aztec ruins and a 12,000-year-old wooly mammoth were discovered. Some of these artifacts are represented in station logos.

The Toronto Subway opened in 1954 as a U-shaped line, which has extended to four routes. The original subway was designed to replace the tram system that traveled the Canadian city's main thoroughfare. In peak hours, trains run every two to three minutes.

The oldest subway in South America is the first of Buenos Aires's subway lines, built in 1913. Known as the Subte, the underground network now has five routes through the Argentine capital, named alphabetically as A, B, C, D, and E lines. In all, there are 69 stations and 26.5 miles (42.7 km) of track.

Built in 1896, the subway in Glasgow is one of the oldest in the world. Its original trains were hauled on a continuous cable, but in 1935 the Scottish subway converted to electric trains. Completing a 6.5-mile (10.4-km) circuit, and with tangerine livery, locals have nicknamed their subway "Clockwork Orange."

In 1966, the overland train network in Oslo, Norway, was connected by tunnels to form the T-bane subway. In 2004, construction caused a tunnel on the busy Grorudbanen line to collapse. The tunnel was rebuilt in six months, relieving streets jammed with replacement buses.

Berlin has an extensive railroad network, part of which, the U-Bahn, runs underground. In 1902, the U-Bahn line opened, with some of its stations situated underground. In the Cold War, when Berlin was divided into East and West Germany, the rail network was also split.

In 1896, Budapest was home to the first electric subway on the European mainland. Situated directly below the Hungarian city's street level and running a 3-mile (5-km) stretch, the original M1 line is just 9 ft (2.75 m) high and 20 ft (6 m) wide.

Tokyo

The first Tokyo subway line opened in 1927 and ran just 1.34 miles (2.2 km) between Ueno and Asakusa. Today, the Japanese city has a thriving subway with 12 busy lines. During rush hour, conductors jam passengers onto packed carriages. Some passengers sleep during their commute, setting their cellphone alarms to wake them at their station.

Paris

In France, Paris's subway pioneered the name the "Métro" when it was built in 1900. In 1956, quieter and fast-accelerating rubber-tired trains—developed by French companies Michelin and Renault—were introduced. Dubbed the "Meteor" when it opened in 1998, the Métro's newest line, Ligne 14, is fully automated.

Moscow

Built in 1935 during Soviet rule, the metro in Moscow has grand marble stations with art, chandeliers, and mosaics. Carrying eight to nine million passengers every day, the Russian subway is the world's busiest. Male staff announce trains running into the city, while female announcers cover those traveling out of Moscow.

○ **St. Petersburg** ○ **Cairo** ○ **Kolkata** ○ **Singapore** ○ **Hong Kong** ○ **Pyongyang** ○ **Melbourne**

The metro in St. Petersburg, Russia, is 70 miles (112 km) long and has 61 stations. Many of these lay as deep as 394 ft (120 m) beneath street level. In the rush hour, trains pass every 95 seconds.

In 1987, the Cairo Metro was the first subway to be built on the African continent. There are two lines, with a third line planned to connect the Egyptian city center to the outlying Cairo airport.

India's first subway, the Kolkata Metro Railway, was built in 1984. It runs for 10 miles (16.5 km), with 17 stations along the route. Each platform is 525 ft (160 m) long.

Platform screen doors help control the climate of Singapore's modern subway, and also protect its commuters. In 2003, automated, driverless trains were introduced.

Of Hong Kong's 50 train stations, 34 are situated underground. Two of the subway lines cross Hong Kong Harbour to service the suburb of Kowloon on the Chinese mainland.

In Pyongyang, North Korea, 17 metro stations lay up to 328 ft (100 m) underground, doubling as nuclear bunkers. The stations have political rather than geographical names.

The rail network in Melbourne is overland, but most suburban trains run an underground circuit called the City Loop. Built in 1984, three subway stations on the Loop service the Australian city's central business district.

Line art

Each of the underground subway systems in cities around the world has its own distinctive design. Whether catching the subway in New York City or the T-bana in Stockholm, colorful signs at street level provide clear directions to the nearest station. The visual display continues underground, with illuminated maps and ticket machines providing information, and sculptures and paintings that make the journey more pleasant.

Denmark: Copenhagen Metro

Singapore: Singapore Metro

Czech Republic: Prague Metro

Russia: Moscow Metro

The Netherlands: Rotterdam Metro

Hong Kong: Hong Kong Metro

Japan: Tokyo Metro

Thailand: Bangkok Metro

Italy: Rome Metro

Austria: Vienna U-Bahn

Belgium: Brussels Metro

Portugal: Lisbon Metro

Japan: Osaka Metro

Argentina: Buenos Aires Metro

Spain: Madrid Metro

Austria: Salzburg U-Bahn

Sweden: Stockholm T-bana

US: Los Angeles Subway

Spain: Barcelona Metro

Greece: Athens Metro

China: Pyongyang Metro

Italy: Naples Metro

Russia: St Petersburg Metro

China: Shanghai Metro

Poland: Warsaw Metro

Egypt: Cairo Metro

Mexico: Mexico City Metro

China: Beijing Subway

Spain: Valencia Metro

France: Paris Metro

Germany: Berlin U-Bahn

Spain: Barcelona Metro

Easy reading

Subway maps have to be clear and easy to read. Most do not accurately represent distances between stations on the ground but instead show the position of the stations in relation to each other on particular lines. Some, like these examples from Beijing, China, and Paris, France, are overlaid on an overground map of the city with streets, rivers, and other features marked on them. You can now download subway maps that can be viewed on a personal MP3 player.

First to set foot

October 12, 1492

The Genoese explorer Christopher Columbus was the first European to set foot on American soil. His fleet landed at a place Columbus called San Salvador. Experts believe this was one of the Bahamas, probably Samana Cay island.

December 14, 1911

The first people to reach the geographic South Pole were part of an expedition led by the Norwegian explorer Roald Amundsen. A British team, led by Robert Falcon Scott, arrived a month later but did not survive.

May 29, 1953

Edmund Hillary of New Zealand and Sherpa Tenzing Norgay of Nepal were the first to reach the peak of Everest. The mountain is the world's tallest, rising 29,015 ft (8,844 m) above sea level. It is part of the towering Himalayan chain.

April 19, 1968

American Ralph Plaisted was the first person to undisputedly set foot on the geographic North Pole. Fellow American Robert Peary believed that he reached it on April 6, 1909, but experts think he was probably a few miles away.

One small step

The first footprints on the Moon were made on July 21, 1969, by American astronaut Neil Armstrong, commander of the *Apollo 11* space mission. Armstrong recognized that it was a historic, symbolic moment. As he stepped out of the *Eagle* landing craft, he announced "That's one small step for man, one giant leap for mankind." The prints from Armstrong's moon boots are still there, and so are the prints of other astronauts who explored the lunar surface. That is because there is no wind on the Moon to blow them away.

The earliest-known samples of hominid (prehuman) footprints were discovered in 1976 in Laetoli, Tanzania. These footprints were made 3.6 million years ago by two upright-walking hominids known as *Australopithecus afarensis*. By examining the trails, experts have figured out that one of the track-makers was large, while the other was small. Some experts argue that the impressions indicate that one of the creatures had an infant resting on its hip. The prehistoric tracks were made in volcanic ash, which became a cementlike substance when wet from rain. Then, following another violent volcanic eruption, the footsteps were preserved in a final layer of ash.

First impressions

A footprint is an extraordinary thing. It is evidence of human life and human traffic. Most footprints are short-lived—they disappear as snow melts or mud is washed away. Footprints last only in extraordinary circumstances, such as the eruption of a volcano or the weatherless conditions of the Moon. When footprints are preserved, they function as talismans, powerful symbols of how humankind as a whole strives, adapts, and survives. In 2003, archeologists working on the Roccamonfina volcano near Naples, southern Italy, found three tracks of footprints preserved in volcanic ash. Made 385,000 to 325,000 years ago, the fossilized prints are the oldest-known *Homo* (human) footprints from an ancient civilization.

On foot

From planes and trains to buses and bikes, there are many forms of transport to get us from place to place, but with all our modern forms of transport, some journeys on Earth can only be undertaken on foot, such as the 29,029-ft (8,848-m) climb to the summit of the world's highest mountain, Mount Everest. Walking is our oldest method of getting around, and sometimes it is simply quicker and more pleasurable to use our feet.

Peak of fitness

Climbing a great mountain is an immense achievement and a perilous adventure. Potential disaster always looms, from the possibility of altitude sickness, hypothermia, and frostbite, to changeable weather conditions, falling rocks, and avalanches. Mountaineers must have the energy to scale the mountain while carrying all of their climbing tools, camping equipment, and food.

Walking wonders

■ In New York City, an estimated total of 6,400 miles (10,300 km) of sidewalks give pedestrians access all over the city.

■ American David Kunst was the first person to walk around the world. The journey took more than four years, and Kunst wore out 21 pairs of shoes crossing four continents and covering 14,447 miles (23,250 km).

■ When mountaineers climb to an altitude of more than 26,247 ft (8,000 m), the reduced oxygen levels decrease their mental performance by 70 percent.

■ In the United Kingdom, the average person walks a total of 200 miles (322 km) each year. Individual journeys are an average distance of 0.6 miles (1 km).

■ Between April 1931 and October 1932, Plennie Wingo walked backward from California to Istanbul, in Turkey. His journey covered 8,000 miles (12,875 km).

City traffic

In congested cities, the quickest way to travel short distances is usually on foot. The world's busiest pedestrian crossing is Hachiko Crossing in Tokyo, Japan. It is estimated that between two to three million people walk across it each day. Every three minutes, road traffic is stopped to make way for the flood of pedestrians.

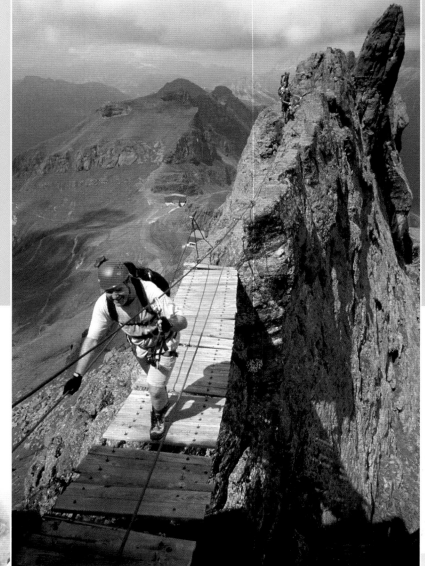

Taking the high route

Throughout the Alps, high-level footpaths known as *Via Ferrata* or *Klettersteig* are fitted with cables, steel ladders, and suspension bridges. Equipped with safety equipment, such as helmets, ropes, and harnesses, hikers can use the paths to reach high pinnacles that would otherwise require advanced rock-climbing skills.

Heavy crowds

When thousands of people gather to walk together, the sea of faces they create is an amazing sight! There are many reasons why people converge to walk in massive groups, from protests and rallies, to cultural parades and religious pilgrimages, such as this gathering in Tibet.

Pedal power

Bicycles have come a long way since the first "boneshakers" rattled along cobblestone streets and unpaved roads in the mid-1800s. Today's bicycles are built in all shapes and sizes to suit all sorts of terrains, from city streets to country tracks. Most bicycles have added gears and suspension to provide a more comfortable ride. Riding a bicycle is a cheap and efficient means of transportation, and is especially convenient when used to cover short distances, or to tour and explore at an easy pace. Cycling is also a popular sport, with riders racing either cross-country or on specially built tracks called velodromes.

Monowheel
This odd-looking vehicle, designed in 2000 by Chinese inventor Li Yongli, is a monowheel. Like a unicycle, a monowheel has just one wheel. The difference is that the rider sits inside the rim of the wheel to control the vehicle. The main wheel is propelled by a series of smaller, pedal-driven wheels.

Chopper
Based on the style for customizing Harley-Davidson motorcycles, the Chopper bicycle has been a cult classic since the 1970s. It has different-sized wheels and high-rise handlebars. One of its most distinctive features is the long, padded seat with a backrest, which provides just enough room for a passenger.

Mountain bike

With high traction tires, a large rounded frame, and added suspension, mountain bikes, such as the Scott Genius RC-10, are built tough to ride through forests and bushland, trek rocky plains, or slide down steep gravel trails. The first mountain bikes were created in the 1970s by off-road biking enthusiasts in California. With dirt motorbikes as their inspiration, they modified 1940s Schwinn bicycles, adding deep-treaded tires and strong brakes. Today, around eight out of 10 bicycles sold are mountain bikes, yet only 10 to 20 percent of these are actually ridden off-road.

Smooth steering

The front wheel on a mountain bike is connected to the frame by forks, which also enable the rider to steer. The quality of the forks directly affects the handling of the mountain bike. The TerraLogic™ forks on the Scott Genius RC-10 can be adjusted to alter the level of suspension. The forks are designed to be stiff when riding a smooth road, but pump into action when riding over rough ground.

Spring suspension

Good suspension provides mountain bikers with a smoother ride on uneven terrain. Inside the forks, spring-loaded shock absorbers help soften the impact from the ground.

1 Force from a bump pushes the slider up.

2 Damping mechanism is activated allowing the oil to pass through a hole. This controls the speed the fork reacts to bumps.

3 Air is compressed by a piston moving up the stanchion absorbing the force of the bump.

4 Spring helps ease the slider as it returns to its starting position.

Stanchion (metal tube)

Compressed air acts as a spring inside the stanchion

Piston

Ultrastiff one-piece slider

Damping mechanism (adjustable valve)

Tightly coiled spring

Oil

Suspension

Suspension activated

Taking it apart

The Scott Genius RC-10 mountain bike is specially built for speed, resilience, and maneuverability, with full suspension, and three levels of shock absorption adjustable to suit every terrain. It has 27-speed gears and hydraulic brakes for better control in different track conditions. The bicycle is made from carbon fiber—an expensive, rust-proof, and lightweight compound that is stronger than steel and is used in the construction of aircraft and space shuttles.

Rear shock linkage plate

Left handlebar grip

Carbon fiber seat post

Carbon fiber frame (front triangle)

Carbon fiber handlebars

Rear wheel

Gear cable

Male saddle

Rear light

Unicycle

Popular with clowns, jugglers, trapeze artists, and stunt performers, a unicycle has just one wheel. Unicycles with extra-tall seat posts are known as "giraffes." It takes practice and balance to be a unicyclist.

Trishaw

A three-wheeled rickshaw, or trishaw, uses pedal power to transport people or goods. This Vietnamese man is driving his family, but trishaws also operate as taxis in southern Asian cities.

Cruiser

A cruiser is built for maximum riding comfort, with laid-back handlebars, and wide, smooth tyres. It also has a padded seat and few or no gears. Some cruisers are specifically built for beach-side rides.

Recumbent bicycle

A rider on a recumbent bike sits back or lies down. Riding in this reclining position is more comfortable than riding a conventional upright bicycle, and places less strain on the back and joints.

Folding bicycle

Many bike manufacturers produce models that fold up. A folding bike takes up less storage space than a conventional one, and it can be carried easily for part of a trip, in a car or on public transportation.

Tandem

Multibicycles carry more than one rider. The two-person tandem is the most common. The challenge for tandem riders is to synchronize their effort, especially if they have different levels of ability.

Racing bicycle

With its lightweight frame, raised seat, dropped handlebars, and narrow, high-pressure tires, a racing bike is superfast. Time-trial bikes like this one have many aerodynamic features to increase speed.

Mountain bicycle

Designed for off-road cycling on tough terrains, mountain bikes have a strong frame, added suspension, and wide, treaded tires. Some mountain bikes have up to 27 gears.

Classic bicycle

There are more than 1,000 million bikes in the world, and most are standard models for everyday use. Popular accessories include a basket to carry goods, and a bell to warn people that the bicycle is approaching.

BMX

Developed for dirt-track racing, BMX (short for "bicycle motocross") bicycles are also ridden freestyle—performing wheelies, jumps, and other tricks. BMX bikes have relatively small wheels—usually 20 in (50 cm) across. Their knobby tires give them an excellent grip on sand, dirt, and slopes.

Rear calliper for hydraulic disk brake

Brake pad set

Rear disk rotor for hydraulic disk brake

Cassette lock ring

11-tooth sprocket for cassette

Inter-sprocket spacer for cassette

16-tooth sprocket for cassette

12-tooth sprocket for cassette

14-tooth sprocket for cassette

Rear quick-release

Rear shock linkage plate

Suspension bolts

Air-sprung rear adjustable suspension

Chain stay protector

Aluminum swing arm (rear triangle)

Main suspension pivot bolt and washers

Bearing

Bottom bracket

Bearing

Rear derailleur to change gears

Gear cassette

Bottom bracket mounted front derailleur to change gears

Chain

Seat

A champion ride
The Scott Genius RC-10 is popular with serious riders and athletes. On the Genius's release in 2003, the bike's success was sealed when racer Thomas Frischknecht rode a Genius to win the marathon distance in the Mountain Bike World Championships in Lugano, Italy.

Stem

Top tube

Head tube

Gear cable

Brake hose

Seat tube

Deep tread tire

Frame anatomy
The triangle is the strongest geometric shape, able to withstand extreme pressure. Two triangles form the standard diamond bike frame. Mountain bike frames are modified to accommodate suspension.

Down tube

Forks

Seat stays

Chain stays

Pedal power
When a rider presses a lever on the handlebar, derailleur gears send the bike chain to "derail" across a series of sprockets into another gear. Gears ease the burden placed on the rider. For example, when climbing hills in a low gear, the rider must pedal more, but can put less pressure on the pedals than if they are riding in a higher gear. The Scott Genius RC-10 gives riders the choice of 27 gears.

Wheel rim

Wheel spoke

Chain

Bolts and washers

Air-sprung suspension fork

Right handlebar grip

Hydraulic brake hose

Crown race to support bearing unit

Lower cartridge bearing

Upper cartridge bearing

Top race

Dual compound tyre for muddy conditions

Remote control adjuster for rear suspension

Carbon fiber spacer

Dual control levers for controlling gears and brakes

Front light

Stem to fix handlebar to frame

Carbon fiber spacer

Top cap

Top cap bolt to secure suspension fork to frame

Crank set

Front calliper for
hydraulic disc
brake

Female seat

Nuts and bolts

Inner tube

Pad securing
bolt

Brake pad

Pad spring

Front quick-
release

Brake pad

Front disc rotor for
disc brake

Left crank
cap

Studs for extra grip on shoes

Velcro-
fastening
shoe

Left clipless
pedal

Cleat to attach
shoe to pedal

Cleat
adapter

Left crank

Mounting
bolts

Right clipless
pedal

Shoe with
cleats and
cross-country
studs

Front wheel

Tour de France

The Tour de France is the world's most famous bicycle race. The route of the race changes annually, traversing France and sometimes entering other European countries. Every July, spectators cheer for their cycling heroes along country roads to Paris's magnificent avenue, the Champs-Élysées. The three-week race is broken into around 20 stages, with 21 teams of nine cyclists competing for the prized *maillot jaune* (yellow jersey).

Tough terrain
Alpe d'Huez is infamous for being an especially long and steep Alpine stage, with an altitude of 6,102 ft (1,860 m). Climbing across 8.6 miles (13.9 km) at a steep gradient, the imposing mountain regularly features as an arduous day in the Tour.

Time trials
Strategically spread across the Tour, three or four time trials see teams and individuals competing against the clock for the fastest race times. Time trials are the only part of the Tour where cyclists are allowed to use aerodynamically designed helmets and handlebars. This streamlined equipment helps cyclists to reach top speeds.

Racing hazards

While bad weather is one hazard that cyclists must contend with, there is also interference from supporters lining the route. Some fans slap riders on the back, wave flags close to the bicycles, throw water, or, most dangerously, leap onto the track. Serious accidents can also occur when cyclists become tangled with one another at high speeds.

Riding in packs

The *peloton* is the French term used to describe the main group of cyclists riding together. Team members work together to set the pace of the *peloton*. The rider who is at the front of the pack will spend several seconds using 100 percent of his pedaling ability until another team member relieves him and takes over the lead.

Winning stages

Cyclists' times are accumulated on a system called the General Classification. The rider ranked first on the General Classification after the final stage of the Tour is the overall winner. If a rider is awarded two jerseys at the same time, he will wear the most prestigious jersey.

Best young rider
The *maillot blanc* (white jersey) is awarded to the best young rider. The rider must be aged under 25 on January 1 of the year of the Tour.

King of the mountains
The *maillot à pois rouge* (white jersey with red polka dots) is awarded to the cyclist who is the best climber across the Tour's mountain stages.

Overall leader
The *maillot jaune* (yellow jersey) is awarded to the rider who accumulates the lowest times in the race. The final overall leader receives this jersey at the podium.

Points leader
The *maillot vert* (green jersey) is awarded to the rider who wins the most points across various stages of the Tour. Good sprinters tend to win this jersey.

City cycling

With urban roads becoming more and more congested, it is little wonder that the number of bicycle commuters is rising. Most use their bikes to travel to and from work, while a few are in the saddle all day as part of their job. The bicycle has many advantages for the city traveler—it costs nothing to run or park, is pollution-free, and it keeps the rider in shape. Cyclists can outpace cars and buses on short journeys because they can avoid traffic jams. Some cities, such as Amsterdam in the Netherlands, have introduced bike-friendly traffic measures to encourage commuters to cycle to work.

Green for go
There are a variety of road signs and traffic measures in place to help cyclists. This traffic light signal means that only bikes can go. After a short time the light turns completely green so that all road traffic facing it can advance. It gives cyclists a useful head start in crossing complicated road intersections.

Lane-free roa
In Vietnam, as in many Asian countries, far more peo travel by bicycle than in cars, buses, or trucks. There are cycle lanes, but often there are no road markings for a kind of traffic. People make their way around the city best they can. Brakes and a loud horn or bell are essenti

In the fast lane
Amsterdam has 176 miles (284 km) of cycle lanes. Most experts think that cycle-only lanes make city cycling safer. They reduce the risk of drivers coming too close and make cyclists less likely to ride on the sidewalk, where they are a danger to pedestrians.

...aving lives

...ndon is one of many cities pioneering the use of paramedic ...ke teams. These paramedics save lives because they can reach ...e scene of an emergency quickly. Carrying a range of first-...d equipment and drugs, the bicycle paramedic assesses and ...abilizes the patient before an ambulance arrives.

...ke patrol

...any police forces have bicycle patrol units. They can cover ...rge areas without getting caught in traffic, which makes them ...ore efficient for patrols or pursuing suspects. Police officers ...trolling on bicycles are easy to approach, which helps them ...build good relationships in the community.

In the post

Soon after the bicycle was invented, it was adopted for delivering mail. In 1896, the British post office bought 100 bicycles. Today, bikes are standard-issue for postal workers around the world, from Japan to the USA. The Swiss postal service alone owns more than 3,700 delivery bikes.

Speedy delivery

In India, cycle rickshaws are often used to transport goods. The rickshaws are cheaper than using a delivery van, and do not add to the air and noise pollution. However, goods can be damaged if there are heavy rains. Some types of rickshaws have electric motors to help drivers turn the pedals.

Dropped handlebars enable more steering positions than upright handlebars.

Shoe straps help the rider grip the pedal.

This bike has a single fixed gear.

Sending messages

Bike messengers carry packages to all parts of New York City, delivering anything from important business documents to gifts. Some bike messengers are so fast and efficient they can deliver up to 40 packages in one working day.

Water and sugary
energy drinks keep
runners hydrated.

Wraparound sunglasses
cut out the sun's glare
and dangerous
ultraviolet rays.

Stopwatches motivate
runners to improve on
their best running times.

Registration numbers are
used to identify runners.

Core-strength exercises,
such as stomach
crunches, give runners
added stamina.

High-tech materials
draw sweat away
from the skin.

Leg-strengthening
exercises enable
runners to move
more efficiently.

Soft, lightweight
racing shoes help
marathon runners
last the distance.

An electronic timing
chip is clipped onto
the shoe to record
official running time.

Marathon

Running a marathon is an epic feat of human endurance, requiring peak physical condition and mental stamina. To complete the arduous 26.2-mile (42.195-km) course, many runners adopt a six-month training schedule involving five or six distance runs each week. Around the world, there are more than 800 marathons held each year. Some marathons, such as those in New York City and London, are so popular that amateur runners must first enter a ballot or lottery system for an opportunity to run in the race.

Burning up

During a marathon, an athlete's liver and muscles convert carbohydrates into a fast-burning energy called glycogen. Glycogen lasts around 20 miles (32 km) before the body burns its fat stores. Runners can then become fatigued, which is known as "hitting the wall."

Start times are
staggered so
elite runners are
not held up by
amateur athletes.

Water stands line
the route to help
runners avoid
dehydration.

Runners drink
diluted sports
gels and special
drinks to build
energy levels.

Half-marathon
races are a good
way to train for
a full marathon.

| mile 01 (1.6 km) | mile 02 (3.2 km) | mile 03 (4.8 km) | mile 04 (6.4 km) | mile 05 (8 km) | mile 06 (9.6 km) | mile 07 (11.3 km) | mile 08 (12.9 km) | mile 09 (14.5 km) | mile 10 (16 km) | mile 11 (17.7 km) | mile 12 (19.3 km) | mile 13 (20.9 km) |

Famous marathons

The world's five most prestigious city marathons are in Berlin, Boston, Chicago, London, and New York City. The biggest marathons are in New York and London. In 2005, 36,856 runners completed the New York Marathon, while 35,260 runners finished London's race.

Race for everyone

On April 21, 1975, the Boston Marathon was the first major marathon to include a wheelchair division. Today's marathons are open to any athlete up to the challenge, whether they are able-bodied or have a disability.

Many runners hit "the wall" when energy levels are at a low.

The name "marathon" comes from an Ancient Greek legend in which a soldier ran 21.4 miles (34.5 km) from the Battle of Marathon to Athens.

The present marathon length was fixed at the 1908 London Olympics, with the start line moved back to give the royal family a better view.

| mile 14 (22.5 km) | mile 15 (24.1 km) | mile 16 (25.7 km) | mile 17 (27.3 km) | mile 18 (28.9 km) | mile 19 (30.6 km) | mile 20 (32.2 km) | mile 21 (33.8 km) | mile 22 (35.4 km) | mile 23 (37 km) | mile 24 (38.6 km) | mile 25 (40.2 km) | mile 26.2 (42.195 km) |

Extreme!

Reaching great heights
A vert ramp is a structure where skateboarders, inline skaters, and BMX riders perform aerial tricks. The flat floor gradually forms a U-shape ending in two vertical walls. Vert ramps are usually more than 10-ft (3-m) tall, with vertical sections of wall measuring up to 3 ft (0.9 m).

Pushing skills to the limit, adrenaline-pumped sports involving speed and thrill-seeking are often dubbed "extreme." Since the 1980s, skateboarding has become a hugely popular recreational activity and means of transportation for young people. Along with skateboarding, extreme sports such as freestyle motocross, inline skating, kite skating, and BMX feature in the Gravity Games and other professional tournaments around the world. Snowboarding is the first extreme sport to become an Olympic event, debuting in the 1998 Winter Olympics in Nagano, Japan.

Getting air
In 1978, 15-year-old Alan Gelfand invented skateboarding's most famous trick, the "ollie." Many tricks, such as this kickflip (pictured), stem from the ollie. Skaters perform an ollie by using their back foot to snap down hard on the tail of the skateboard, while sliding their front foot forward. Seemingly defying gravity, the board can be maneuvered by the skater midflight.

Kite skating

Propelled along by wind-powered kites, kite skaters require wide surfaces such as beaches, empty parking lots, or open fields to perform their sport. Since kites are involved, it is important that both the air and ground space are not obstructed. Some kite skaters choose to ride four-wheeled mountain boards (pictured), while others use off-road inline skates, fitted with large, high-traction wheels.

Inline skating

Using skates equipped with four or five wheels positioned in a single line, inline skaters ride on many of the same terrains as skateboarders. "Aggressive skating" is a type of inline street skating in which skaters perform dramatic jumps and tricks, such as grinding (riding on handrails down stairs). Some people inline skate without brakes, while others use a stop located on the heel of one skate.

Street luge

Torpedoing down steep mountain roads in a horizontal position, street luge racers can reach high speeds of 80 mph (130 km/h). Riders must wear motorcycle helmets and leather safety gear for protection. Street luge boards are sometimes custom-made, built from carbon fiber, steel, wood, or aluminum. Riders steer their luge boards by leaning their bodies to the left or right.

Snowboarding

"Freestyle" is one of the most popular forms of snowboarding, where riders perform tricks similar to those done on skateboards. Some ski fields have designated areas with jumps for boarders. As with skateboarding, snowboarders who place their right foot forward on the board are known as "goofy", while "regular" riders ride with their left foot to the front.

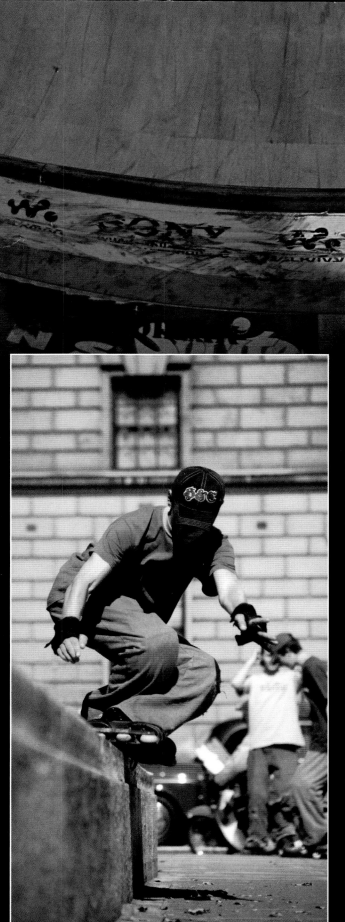

Off the kerb

Whether they are riding on inline skates or a skateboard, many street skaters use public facilities to perform their tricks, such as curbs, steps, and handrails. Urban skateparks have these facilities specially built for street skaters in a safer environment.

Snow motion

Snow and ice can bring chaos to the roads, even in parts of the world that are used to severe weather conditions. The principal challenge is to stay upright! Wheels are not designed for traveling over a surface that has almost no friction. They need help in the form of treaded tires or snow chains. On highways and main roads, there are usually measures to clear the snow altogether, such as sanders or snowplows. Skis, sleds, and snowmobiles are a practical way to travel over snow, because they rest on runners that simply slide across the slippery surface.

Tire chains

In mountainous, snowy areas, such as the Alps or the Rockies, cars may have to use snow chains to drive in the icy conditions. These chains are attached to the wheels and help prevent dangerous skidding. They are especially useful in the mountains, where roads have tight turns that can be hidden by huge snowdrifts.

Driving on ice

Four-wheel-drive vehicles have more traction on ice than cars in which only the front wheels are powered, but all drivers can minimize skidding. To slow down, drivers should ease pressure off the accelerator. Braking hard can result in loss of control.

Clearing roads

Spreading a sand and salt mixture on main roads and busy sidewalks is common practice wherever freezing conditions are forecast. The salt helps ice and snow melt more quickly and the sand gives tires something to grip in the meantime. In serious blizzards, snowplows have to clear the roads.

Snowshoes

Strapped over ordinary shoes, snowshoes help people walk through snow without slipping or sinking. There is evidence that people have made them for thousands of years. The racket-shaped frame that surrounds a lattice of leather or string is designed not to collect snow.

Traveling by sled

Traditionally, people living in the Arctic cross snowy terrain by sled—vehicles that slide along ski-like runners rather than rolling on wheels. Sleds are made of wood and are usually pulled along by reindeer or husky dogs. They can transport goods or people over the ice at high speeds.

City skiing

During the blizzard of 2003, some New Yorkers moved around the city on skis. The storm was a freak event but in some places, such as Scandinavian countries, skiing is still used as a practical means of travel. Cross-country skiing originated in Norway in the 1800s. Early skis were made of wood, while today's are usually fiberglass.

Snowmobile
Motorized sleds, called snowmobiles, are especially popular in the northern US states, Alaska, and Canada, where snow can lie on the ground for many months of the year. They have skis, a gasoline engine, and can travel across ice at speeds of 45 mph (72 km/h).

Emergency

"Emergency!" is written in reverse on medical response vehicles, so drivers can see the word correctly in their rear-view mirrors and know to pull over, allowing them to pass. Many emergency services vehicles have flashing lights and a loud siren to warn people in the vicinity that their journey is urgent. These public service teams include police, paramedics, and firefighters. Depending on the location of the situation and the type of emergency reported, response teams can arrive at the scene in anything from a huge truck to a sportscar.

Arriving in style

Traffic police in Italy have use of a high-speed Lamborghini car. The equipment inside the vehicle includes direct connection to police databases, technology to record violations, and a scanner for license plate recognition.

Access all areas

Smart cars are used by police in countries such as the Czech Republic and UK. These compact cars have room for a police officer and emergency equipment, and are small enough to safely zip around city streets.

Speedy service

Motorbike ambulances can reach emergency situations much faster than their van counterparts. As well as weaving through traffic jams, motorbikes save time by stopping at the scene instead of parking somewhere first.

Mobile medication

Larger ambulances, such as this Japanese camper van, have a driver and at least one paramedic at every emergency. These vehicles have the equipment to stabilize a sick or injured patient's condition during the trip to hospital.

First ambulances: Horse-drawn ambulances during American Civil War, 1861–65   **Largest ambulance service:** London, UK, with 1.5 million patients a year   **Biggest ambulance:** 59-ft- (18-m-) long Alligator Jumbulances, UK

Fire extinguishers
When a blaze is reported, a fire engine is sent from an emergency dispatch center to put out the flames. Fire trucks, such as this one in Indiana, have a large on-board water supply, which can be pumped through hoses managed by the firefighters. Fire engines also carry ladders, axes, and breathing apparatus.

KOKOMO FIRE DEPT.

Largest volunteer ambulance service: Abdul Sattar Edhi, Pakistan, with 500 ambulances   **First fire station:** Ancient Rome in 24 BCE   **Average cost of a new, fully equipped fire engine:** More than $435,000

Trucking

Around the clock, trucks of all shapes and sizes freight anything from livestock to flammable substances. Some drivers own their truck, while others drive company-owned vehicles. A driver's job includes keeping detailed log books, loading and unloading cargo, changing heavy tires, and having a good knowledge of mechanics. Some truck cabins have a small bed for the driver to sleep on after driving long distances.

Overload!

Usually, trucks must comply with strict load limits. However, this truck driver in Somalia, Africa, seems to have ignored any safety rules. The truck is overloaded with harvested corn.

Kings of the road

In the Australian outback, trucks known as road trains lug three or more trailers of goods over long distances between remote towns. The long and heavy multiple trailers make road trains difficult to maneuver, and suitable only for driving on flat stretches of road that are mostly free of traffic.

Mining giant

Towering at more than 22 ft (6.7 m) tall, huge dump trucks shift hundreds of tons of dirt, rocks, and mining materials from quarries and open-pit mines.

Loaded with logs

Log trucks transport felled timber between the forests and sawmills for processing. The timber must be carefully secured to the trailer. Trucks that are used to haul logs are around 98.4 ft (30 m) long.

Trawling tanks

Tankers are trucks with in-built tanks to transport oil, gas, flammable liquids, and other chemicals. Trucks carrying hazardous materials are clearly labeled with their contents in case of an accident or emergency.

Decorative drive

In Pakistan, trucks are ornately painted and carved with designs specific to different regions of the country. Many of these trucks have lucky charms, such as an old shoe, hanging from the bumper.

Moving house

In some parts of the USA, you may spot a small house being moved on a truck! Trucks that carry such homes must drive very slowly to support their unwieldy load.

Monster trucks

With names like Grave Digger, Predator, and Avenger, monster trucks are fearsome beasts designed for maximum destruction. To cheering audiences, these terrifying vehicles race around dirt-filled arenas, crushing cars, small planes, and mobile homes with unrelenting force. Monster trucks are supercharged, custom-built vehicles equipped with mammoth 5.6-ft (1.7-m) tires weighing a hefty 9,000 lb (4,082 kg) or more.

Transformer robot
Transforming from a truck into a 39-ft- (12-m-) tall fire-breathing robotic dinosaur, Robosaurus is an engineering marvel. As it crushes cars in its claws and pulverizes planes in its jaws, Robosaurus mirrors the body movements of its driver, who is connected to high-tech sensors.

Monster racing

Thanks to massive 1,500–2,000 horsepower engines, monster trucks can race short distances at speeds of 100 mph (161 km/h). Common events include "side-by-side" racing where two trucks simultaneously negotiate a track to the finish line, and "freestyle," in which trucks are awarded points for stunts.

Heavy-duty action

Whether they are leaping 25 ft (7.5 m) through the air or performing pogos (bouncing on rear wheels), wheelies (rising on rear wheels), or cyclones (performing high-speed spins), monster trucks need serious suspension. Most monster trucks are fitted with two massive coiled shock absorbers per tire. Over one year, the punishing work of an average monster truck will have destroyed eight sets of tires.

Crushing force

The vehicles crushed by monster trucks are usually purchased from scrap dealers. Built to destroy virtually any obstacle in their path, monster trucks are fitted with a Remote Ignition Interruptor (RII) emergency switch to stop out-of-control trucks from crossing safety barriers and careering into onlookers.

The original monster truck

Big Foot is the original monster truck —a souped-up Ford F-250 4x4 pickup built to promote an American four-wheel-drive business in the late 1970s. Crushing its first car in 1981, Big Foot has spawned 16 generations of "big feet" and popularized the sport of monster trucking around the world.

Offroad

Navigating offroad terrain demands a specialist vehicle and a particular set of driving skills. For some people, driving offroad is a necessity because they work in areas where the roads are in a poor condition—or even nonexistent. Others go offroad for recreation, enjoying the challenge of trying to get their vehicle up a steep mountainside or across a deep river. Whatever the reason, driving offroad can be a thrilling experience.

Treacherous mud
A major problem of driving in mud is that it is unpredictable. Lowering the tire pressures can help, especially when driving though sticky mud. It is important that the vehicle stays in one gear and maintains a steady speed to avoid getting stuck.

Offroad trivia

■ Many offroad vehicles incorporate four-wheel drive. This means that power goes to all four wheels rather than just the two front or rear wheels. It gives the vehicle extra control when driving over difficult terrain.

■ Some offroaders have special "low-ratio" gearboxes. Like the smaller cogs on a bicycle, these allow the vehicle to drive up steeper slopes than would be possible to negotiate with a standard gearbox.

■ The best-known offroad cars are British-made Land Rovers and US-made Jeeps. Both were first manufactured more than 60 years ago and have a reputation for strength and durability.

■ Other forms of vehicles that can be rented from special centers to tackle offroad terrain include trucks, motorbikes, quad bikes, and snowplows. It is even possible to experience offroad driving in a tank.

Slippery snow

Tires are the most important consideration when driving on snow and ice. Chunky tires with deep treads are the best type because they secure the strongest grip. Tire chains can also be used. Gentle braking is a key driving skill, otherwise the wheels will lock and skid.

Precarious water

Driving through water can be extremely treacherous, especially in potentially deep river crossings. If in any doubt, drivers should avoid crossing a river, otherwise the vehicle could get stuck or even be swept away by strong currents. A low gear is selected before entering the water because changing gear while in it will cause loss of momentum.

Dangerous dunes

Wide tires are necessary to negotiate massive sand dunes, such as those found in the Namibian desert in Africa. This is because the vehicle has to virtually "float" over the surface of the sand and not sink down into it. Driving in dunes requires very specialized skills and can be dangerous because the vehicle can easily roll over.

Unpredictable savanna

As well as animal hazards such as cheetahs and lions, offroad safari vehicles often encounter terrain that features ridges that were formed, and rocks that were deposited, during the rainy season. Drivers drive slowly to avoid these obstacles.

The route of the Dakar is notoriously difficult, and the race is considered an endurance test. Thick mud, dangerous rocks, and sand dunes all feature along the way, pushing drivers to their limits.

Dakar Rally

When French rally racer Thierry Sabine got lost in the Libyan desert in 1978, he decided that the desolate landscape would be ideal for a rally—a race across rough land and public roads, with rules governing route, time, and speed. The next year, the Dakar Rally was born. This annual rally includes competitive sections known as "Stages" or "Specials." The noncompetitive route to the start of a Special is called a "Liaison."

Motorbike class
The bike category is one of three classes. KTM is the most popular bike, followed by Yamaha. Participants in this category have to look out for uneven ruts made by trucks as these can cause accidents.

Car class
Volkswagen, Mitsubishi, and Nissan are the leaders in the car class, but entries can vary from small trucks to buggies. Frenchman Jean-Louis Schlesser has won the race twice with his custom-made dune buggies.

Truck class
In recent years, Tatra, DAF, Kamaz, and Mercedes-Benz have been the trucks to watch. Some manufacturers use the rally to test the durability of their new trucks, which are often heavily modified to cope with the tough conditions.

Rally route 2005
The route is one of the longest in the world and includes parts of Europe and Africa. Between Barcelona and Dakar, the distances competitors travel vary from a few miles to a few hundred miles each day. Most of the racers taking part are amateur. In 2005, there were a total of

PORTUGAL

SPAIN

Barcelona 1 2

Granada 3

LEG 1	12.31.04 Barcelona > Barcelona
	Special: 4 miles (6 km)
	Liaisons: 27 miles (44 km)

This was the opening stage of the 2005 Dakar. Known as the Super Special, it established the starting order for the next day. The competitive part took place on the beach.

LEG 2	01.01.05 Barcelona > Granada
	Noncompetitive leg
	Liaison: 572 miles (920 km)

A ceremony was held in Barcelona to introduce the competitors, who then faced a long, grueling drive on the highways to Granada. There was no Special in this leg.

LEG 3	01.02.05 Granada > Rabat
	Special: 6 miles (10 km)
	Liaisons: 350 miles (563 km)

Before leaving Spain, the racers drove a fast and furious 6-mile (10-km) track on military land near Granada. There was a boat crossing at Algeciras before a smooth run in Africa.

LEG 4	03.01.05 Rabat > Agadir
	Special: 76 miles (123 km)
	Liaisons: 337 miles (543 km)

This new African Special was littered with traps. Racers passed a cork oak forest, and then the route got difficult as random changes in direction vexed even experienced drivers.

LEG 5	04.01.05 Agadir > Smara
	Special: 237 miles (381 km)
	Liaisons: 170 miles (273 km)

A warm-up session on a tarmac road to Guelmin prepared the racers for the long Special to follow. High speeds were possible until the terrain became too rocky.

LEG 6	01.05.05 Smara > Zouerat
	Special: 410 miles (660 km)
	Liaison: 5.5 miles (9 km)

After a long, straight run to the Mauritanian border, the tricky African sand dunes gave the competitors the opportunity to show off their navigational skills.

MOROCCO

Agadir 5

Smara 6

WESTERN SAHARA

MAURITANA

MALI

Zouerat 7

11 Atar 10

9 Tidjikja

8 Tichit

Kiffa 12

16 Dakar

14 Kayes

15 Tambacounda

13 Bamako

SENEGAL

GUINEA

Final check

About 485 vehicles are entered in the Dakar. These all need to be safety-checked to ensure they meet the strict regulations of the event, such as wheel size, speed limit, and the compulsory inclusion of a safety horn.

7
Special: 410 miles (660 km)
Liaison: 5.5

As most of the route was new for 2005, previous experience of the rally did not benefit the racers. This leg included fields and camel grass, as well as a tricky cliff pass.

LEG 8 01.07.05 Tichit > Tidjikja
Special: 323 miles (520 km)
Liaison: 11 miles (18 km)

This was one of the most exciting legs and included stretches from the best Specials of the last 20 years. There were challenging sand dunes to cross on the way to the Nega pass.

LEG 9 01.08.05 Tidjikja > Atar
Special: 224 miles (361 km)
Liaisons: 24 miles (38 km)

This was the final stage before the drivers enjoyed a well-earned rest day. They raced along 300 km (186 miles) of track, before problematic dunes forced them to slow down.

LEG 10 01.10.05 Atar > Atar
Special: 300 miles (483 km)
Liaisons: 10 miles (16 km)

Traditionally, the first stretch after rest day is an easy one. But, in 2005, it was the rally's most difficult sand crossing. The racers traveled on to the Thaga pass.

LEG 11 01.11.05 Atar > Kiffa
Special: 408 miles (656 km)
Liaisons: 24 miles (39 km)

To mark the last day in Mauritania, drivers had to navigate an extended Special of 373 miles (600 km). The first half involved soft dunes, while the second crossed an oasis.

LEG 12 01.12.05 Kiffa > Bamako
Special: 364 miles (586 km)
Liaisons: 145 miles (233 km)

Dense vegetation surrounded this route, making landmarks hard to spot and navigation difficult. Drivers passed through villages and rivers, and even spotted some animals along the way.

LEG 13 01.13.05 Bamako > Kayes
Special: 364 miles (586 km)
Liaisons: 145 miles (233 km)

When the drivers reached this Special, they traveled at top speed because the route was clear. The speed dropped at the Manantali barrage—from here on it was bushland.

LEG 14 01.14.05 Kayes > Tambacounda
Special: 317 miles (510 km)
Liaison: 2 miles (3 km)

The track followed the Senegalese border and narrowed the nearer it got to the Faleme River. This historic spot marks the arrival and finish of the rally in Senegal.

LEG 15 01.15.05 Tambacounda > Dakar
Special: 14 miles (22 km)
Liaisons: 214 miles (344 km)

Competitors traveled a long, tarmac road to the next Special, where the dramatic landscape alternated between tropical forest and rough grassland.

LEG 16 01.16.05 Dakar > Dakar
Special: 19 miles (31 km)
Liaison: 23 miles (37 km)

The outcome of the race was already decided for most competitors. In the Dakar tradition, the final Special was a line-up start on the beach. A prize-giving ceremony ended the rally.

青藏铁路工程

青藏铁路

Under construction
About 342 miles (550 km) of the rail route crosses permafrost (permanently frozen ground). Workers lowered stretches of track into place on top of the ice.

Completed in 2006, the Qinghai-Tibet Railroad is a miracle of engineering. It reaches across China from Xining, in the northwestern province of Qinghai, to Lhasa, capital of Tibet. It is the first time that Tibet has been linked to the rest of China. Most of the railroad's 1,180-mile (1,900-km) length is more than 13,125 ft (4,000 m) above sea level. For five months of the year, temperatures along the route drop to –22°F (–30°C).

Railroad in the clouds

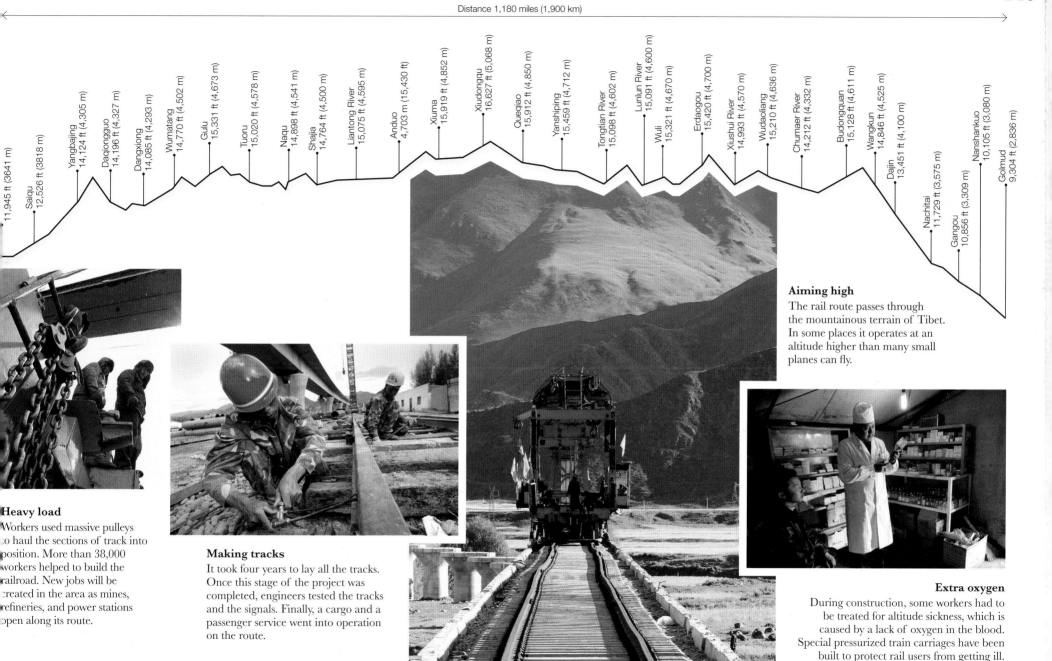

Distance 1,180 miles (1,900 km)

11,945 ft (3641 m)
Saiqu 12,526 ft (3818 m)
Yangbajing 14,124 ft (4,305 m)
Daqiongguo 14,196 ft (4,327 m)
Dangxiong 14,085 ft (4,293 m)
Wumatang 14,770 ft (4,502 m)
Gulu 15,331 ft (4,673 m)
Tuoru 15,020 ft (4,578 m)
Naqu 14,898 ft (4,541 m)
Shajia 14,764 ft (4,500 m)
Liantong River 15,075 ft (4,595 m)
Anduo 4,703 m (15,430 ft)
Xiuma 15,919 ft (4,852 m)
Xiudongqu 16,627 ft (5,068 m)
Queqiao 15,912 ft (4,850 m)
Yanshiping 15,459 ft (4,712 m)
Tongtian River 15,098 ft (4,602 m)
Lunlun River 15,091 ft (4,600 m)
Wuli 15,321 ft (4,670 m)
Erdaogou 15,420 ft (4,700 m)
Xiushui River 14,993 ft (4,570 m)
Wudaoliang 15,210 ft (4,636 m)
Chumaer River 14,212 ft (4,332 m)
Budongquan 15,128 ft (4,611 m)
Wangkun 14,846 ft (4,525 m)
Dajin 13,451 ft (4,100 m)
Nachitai 11,729 ft (3,575 m)
Gangou 10,856 ft (3,309 m)
Nanshankuo 10,105 ft (3,080 m)
Golmud 9,304 ft (2,836 m)

Heavy load

Workers used massive pulleys to haul the sections of track into position. More than 38,000 workers helped to build the railroad. New jobs will be created in the area as mines, refineries, and power stations open along its route.

Making tracks

It took four years to lay all the tracks. Once this stage of the project was completed, engineers tested the tracks and the signals. Finally, a cargo and a passenger service went into operation on the route.

Aiming high

The rail route passes through the mountainous terrain of Tibet. In some places it operates at an altitude higher than many small planes can fly.

Extra oxygen

During construction, some workers had to be treated for altitude sickness, which is caused by a lack of oxygen in the blood. Special pressurized train carriages have been built to protect rail users from getting ill.

Great rail journeys

All aboard! Some rail journeys are famous for their luxurious trains, while others are celebrated for the awe-inspiring scenery they pass. Whether experienced in an opulent first-class berth or a basic economy-class seat, a great rail journey is a nostalgic return to an old-world style of travel. A train can take days to cross states and continents, rather than a few hours spent on a plane. Chugging through desert, forest, or snow, trains enable passengers to make the most of their journey, by enjoying the landscape and stopping off at locations en route.

The great Siberian
Crossing Russia and traveling into Mongolia and China, the Trans-Siberian Railroad is the world's longest railroad. The famed 5,772-mile (9,288-km) journey from Moscow to Vladivostok takes seven days, passing through eight time zones.

The opulent Orient Express
Famed for its first-class luxury, the glamorous Venice Simplon-Orient-Express travels through Europe, visiting Istanbul, London, Paris, Prague, Venice, and Vienna.

Camel of the outback

Named after the Afghan camel caravans used to transport early Australian explorers, the Ghan travels 1,851 miles (2,979 km) between Adelaide and Darwin. Riding deep into the outback, the Ghan traverses red, barren desert as it makes its way toward Australia's steamy, tropical north.

Adventure in the Andes

The many wonders of the ancient Incan civilization can be viewed from a single railroad trip. PeruRail travels between Cuzco, Lake Titicaca, the Sacred Valley, Arequipa, and the ruins of the ancient citadel, Machu Picchu.

Himalayan steam

India's World Heritage-listed Darjeeling Himalayan railroad travels 53 miles (86 km) from Darjeeling to New Jalpaiguri. Steam locomotives have run on the railway since it opened in 1881.

Mountain marvels

In seven-and-a-half hours, Switzerland's Glacier Express connects Zermatt and St. Moritz. The highest peak on the 169-mile (272-km) journey through the Swiss Alps is the Oberalp Pass at 6,670 ft (2,033 m).

South Africa's little gem

Ushering its passengers in five-star comfort through South Africa's famed diamond-mining regions, the Blue Train's regular route is the 994-mile (1,600-km) journey between Pretoria and Cape Town.

Lap of luxury

Traveling through Thailand, Malaysia, and Singapore, the Eastern and Orient Express provides the finest in silver service. On board, the train's cuisine rivals that of the world's best restaurants.

Making tracks

The *Train à Grande Vitesse* (TGV) is a high-speed train that connects many large cities in France. It travels on a specially built network of tracks that enables it to reach speeds of up to 199 mph (320 km/h). Variations of the train also operate in the Netherlands, Spain, and the UK, where Eurostar services through the Channel Tunnel use adapted TGVs.

Ventilation slots provide air cooling for the electronic resistors that heat up when the driver slows down the TGV at high speed.

The TGV has four motors in the front power car (carriage) and a further four in the rear car each of which provides power directly to the wheels.

The auxiliary power unit generates the power for the nontraction parts of the TGV, such as carriage lighting and motor cooling fans.

The main transformer takes the overhead power supply and converts it so that it can then be used to drive the power units.

The pantograph obtains electric current from the overhead lines. All TGVs have one at the front of the train and one at the back.

The impact absorption block provides a protective barrier in the event of a collision, though there have been no fatal crashes in the TGV's history.

An automated system in the cab reads signals that are transmitted through sensors in the track, so easing the workload on the driver.

Each of the two power cars can produce just under 6,000 brake horsepower (a measurement of power) and weighs about 68 tons.

At high speeds, the motor gets very hot and is cooled by freon – a gas that is also used in fridges and air-conditioning systems

The frame upon which the motors are positioned is made of high-grade steel that is both light and strong

Each carriage has two pairs of wheels at the front and two at the rear. The thrust is transmitted through the wheels in the two power cars.

The suspension system is made up of primary and secondary springs, though more recent TGVs use air-filled suspension units

Every carriage incorporates a large luggage compartment, and some TGVs allow bicycles to be transported.

TGVs on each line have different carriage arrangements—the TGV Atlantique is made up of two power cars and ten passenger carriages.

The TGV can operate in other countries where the power current in the overhead cables is different to that found in France.

A typical ten-carriage TGV Atlantique, will include 13 restrooms, plus separate baby-changing facilities.

In 1990, a shortened TGV Atlantique set a world record speed for a conventional train of 320 mph (515 km/h).

The frames upon which the axle, wheels, suspension, gearing, and brake components are mounted are called bogies.

On the TGV Atlantique, there are three first-class carriages, which are usually located at the front of the train.

The TGV Atlantique can seat 465 passengers, but the double-decker TGV Duplex is able to accommodate up to 1,024 people.

The high-tech nature of the train and track means that passengers sitting in a TGV carriage experience a vibration-free, quiet journey.

While the TGV is designed to run on specially constructed high-speed track, it can also operate on normal lines, but at lower speeds.

The commuters

A constant stream of commuters pours through Grand Central Terminal 24 hours a day. Arriving on Metro-North Railroad trains from towns north of New York City, many passengers continue their journeys from the terminal's busy subway station.

Jeremy and Michael

Jeremy loves trains and enjoys visiting Grand Central Terminal with his father, Michael. "In New York, subways are a part of life," says Michael. "We take the subway to go shopping, visit our friends, or go on exciting adventures!"

Tolga and Oliver

Tolga and Oliver are British actors visiting New York for a movie premiere. "We bought one-day passes for $7. The subway makes it easy to travel all over the city."

Jitendra and Gurmeet

"There is a lot of history behind Grand Central. It's a unique place, and it's very efficient, too—I cannot remember having to wait too long for the trains. It's well organized."

Isao and friends

"We are coffee-shop managers from Tokyo visiting New York City on a business trip. Later, we will take the subway to West 60th Street. Now we are eating crêpes and drinking coffee!"

Michael

"When I'm in the New York area, I often take trains to Boston and Washington, DC. I much prefer trains to planes because it's a more comfortable and easy-going journey."

Lining the platform

Grand Central Terminal has 44 platforms where suburban and long-distance trains stop between 5.30 a.m. and 1.30 a.m. every day. Spanning two levels, the platforms service 67 tracks—41 are on the top level and 26 are on the lower level.

Terminal trivia

- Grand Central Terminal stretches across 49 acres (0.2 sq km) and is one of the world's largest train stations.
- 125,000 people commute through the terminal each day.

- 570,000 people visit the terminal each day to shop, sightsee, or eat in the restaurants and cafés.
- Ninety-eight percent of trains arrive at Grand Central Terminal on schedule.

- More than 660 Metro-North trains serve the terminal daily, while trains pass through the terminal's subway station every few minutes.
- There are 25 automated ticket vending machines located throughout the terminal.

- 30,000 bulbs are used to light Grand Central Terminal each year.
- More than five tons of newspapers are collected throughout the terminal for recycling every day.

Famed for its architecture, Grand Central Terminal in
New York City is both an icon for the city and a symbol
of the railroad. It is a bustling transportation hub, with more
than half a million people passing through each day.
Trains arrive from and depart to towns in New York State
and Connecticut, and the subway station is the city's busiest.

Grand Central Terminal
New York City

Walking the marble floor
Filled with commuters and visitors
moving in every direction, the
terminal's main concourse is
200 ft (61 m) long. Light pours
into the terminal through the
three 60-ft- (18-m-) high
arched windows.

The workers

Grand Central Terminal provides jobs for more than one thousand people. Some work on the trains as engineers and conductors, or help customers at the information desks. Others are employed in the terminal's shops and restaurants.

Luis

Luis is a police officer patrolling the terminal. "I make sure that everything is safe, secure, and running smoothly. Every day is different. Some days I help sick or injured people, but mostly I answer people's questions."

Pat

"I inspect tickets, answer questions, and ensure passengers get on and off the train safely. I also help decide how many carriages we need on the train," explains Pat, a conductor on the New Haven line.

Tom

Tom is the automated ticket sales manager at the terminal. "There are around 7,000 tickets in each vending machine. Most ticket machines are restocked every two or three weeks."

Bill

As a locomotive simulator technician, Bill operates computers that new engineers use to practice driving trains. "It's important that student engineers are familiar with the cab and using the controls before driving a real train."

Mike

Mike works in the terminal's very busy lost property office, which recovers 19,000 items each year. "A strange time was when we had three people looking for two sets of false teeth. One guy wanted to try them all out!"

Audrey

In the Center Information Booth, customer services manager Audrey is asked up to 1,000 questions an hour. "We can refer to computers and information boards, but the answers soon become second nature!"

Keeping on track

- Established in 1913, the Oyster Bar serves more than 20,000 oysters every day.
- Proposing marriage in the Whispering Gallery next to the Oyster Bar is a New York City tradition.

- More than 10,000 meals are served in the terminal's cafes and restaurants each day.
- A master clock synchronizes all of the terminal's clocks to ensure accuracy up to one-billionth of a second.

- 60 rail traffic controllers direct trains on the lines that enter and leave the terminal.
- 100 conductors stamp tickets, collect fares, and assist passengers to safely board and exit Metro-North trains.

- 50 cleaners work shifts throughout the extensive terminal.
- Transit Bureau, a division of the New York Police Department, patrols Grand Central Terminal and the greater rail network.

0 — 60

Start your engines! With pedals to the metal, motor races are charged with high-octane atmosphere. Tires squeal and rubber burns in the quest for the checkered flag. In the United States, NASCAR, IndyCar, and top-fuel drag racing reign supreme, while in Europe and much of Asia, the number one motorsport championships are the Formula One Grand Prix and MotoGP grand prix series.

Formula One (F1) Grand Prix

F1 is the top class of motor racing, and the world's most expensive sport. Race teams compete for the Drivers' and Constructors' World Championships each year. Since 1984, the Ferrari, McLaren, Renault, and Williams teams have dominated the F1 championships.

NASCAR (National Association for Stock Car Auto Racing)

Exceeding 200 mph (322 km/h), NASCARs are high-powered racing cars fitted with thin sheet-metal bodies to look like stock (road) cars. In North America, dozens of tracks host more than 100 races each year. The largest NASCAR competitions are the Nextel Cup, the Busch Series, and the Craftsman Truck Series.

Motorcycle Grand Prix (MotoGP)

With an annual series of 17 rounds in 15 countries, each Motorcycle Grand Prix race lasts just 45 minutes without pit stops. Powered by 60 cu in four-stroke engines, MotoGP bikes have technology unavailable on road-going motorcycles.

IndyCar

Fitted with methanol engines, IndyCars produce more than 650 horsepower, going from 0–60 mph (0–96.5 km/h) in less than three seconds. The most famous IndyCar event is the Indianapolis 500, where drivers cover 200 laps of the 2.5-mile (4.02-km) circuit, equaling 500 miles (804.6 km).

McLaren F1

Launched in 1993, the super-exotic McLaren F1 is one of the fastest cars to go on sale to the public. With only 100 cars manufactured, the McLaren F1 is also one of the most expensive road cars, costing around $1,105,765. Equipped with a 1.3-gallon (6.1-liter) V12 BMW engine, the McLaren F1 has a maximum speed of 240 mph (386.4 km/h).

Rallycross

Audiences lining the safety barriers at a rallycross event eagerly await excitement-packed racing. In rallycross, rivals race each other across tarmac roads and muddy tracks. Rallycross cars look like their regular road counterparts, such the Ford Focus, yet they are custom-built, hi-tech racing monsters!

Top-fuel drag racing

Soaring along a 0.25-mile (400-m) strip in under 4.5 seconds, a top-fuel dragster is powered by 85 percent nitromethane and 15 percent methanol (racing alcohol). Rocketing to 280 mph (450 km/h) in 656 ft (200 m), dragsters are equipped with parachutes to help them slow down. Before a run, drivers must warm their tires by spinning them in a spectacular "burn out."

Front forks provide suspension as they move by up to 11.8 in (30 cm) to absorb impact.

The front mudguard prevents mud thrown up from the wheel from obscuring the rider's view.

Stunt show

It's show time and you've got a front-row seat! This action-packed motorcycle show stars ex-world championship motocross rider Jason Smyth. Motocross involves motorcycle racing over tough, cross-country terrain, and this is where the stuntman learnt his tricks. He now performs a range of heart-stopping feats at locations around Europe, adapting his display to the size of each venue. In small 165 ft (50 m) by 65 ft (20 m) arenas, minibikes are ridden, while at larger sites more powerful 250cc machines can be used.

Shin guards, knee
braces, and padded
pants protect the
lower half of the body.

Muffler at the end of the
exhaust pipe muffles
the engine noise.

Breather and overflow
pipes prevent the engine
flooding during stunts.

Soft, strong tires provide
maximum grip when
landing on ramps.

Motocross cycles

Today, the most popular form
of amateur motorcycle racing
is motocross. The bikes are
lightweight and geared for rapid
acceleration rather than continual top
speeds. Due to the number of tricky
landings, the suspension system is highly
absorbent, and a long saddle covers the
fuel tank to protect the rider.

Catching the rings

This stunt relies on accurate judgment of distance.
The stuntman builds up a speed of 40 mph (64 km/h), before
mounting a starting ramp and taking off. The distance between
the starting ramp and the landing ramp is about 80 ft (25 m).
Between the ramps is a pole with rings attached to it. The stuntman
catches these rings 30 ft (9 m) up in the air before landing hands-free
on a ramp, which is covered in mesh to maximize grip.

Stand-up wheelie

The stuntman crashes most often during
ground stunts. The KTM SX 250 bike
is used because it has soft suspension
and hand guards. Speeds of up to 50 mph
(80 km/h) are reached during wheelies.

One-handed stoppie

When the stuntman rides only on
the front wheel, it is called a "stoppie."
Regularly performing stoppies causes
huge pressure on the wheels. They buckle
under the strain and have to be replaced.

Cool rides

From thrilling rides on open country roads to winding in and out of jammed peak-hour traffic, motorcycles provide riders with a cheaper, cooler, and less cumbersome alternative to driving a car. While motorcycles are often used as a means of everyday transportation, there are also many that take pride of place in their owner's garage, reserved for special rides on the weekends and vacations. Serious enthusiasts choose their bikes based on their high performance, fine styling, and collectability. Whether it is a classic Norton, Ducati, Triumph, or Harley-Davidson, for some collectors money is no object when it comes to buying their dream machine.

BAT, 1904
Top speed: 25 mph (40 km/h)
Power: 500 cc
Country of origin: UK

Indian 1914 V-Twin, 1914
Top speed: 55 mph (89 km/h)
Power: 1000 cc
Country of origin: US

Ace, 1919
Top speed: 65 mph (105 km/h)
Power: 1229 cc
Country of origin: US

Megola Racing Model, 1923
Top speed: 68 mph (109 km/h)
Power: 640 cc
Country of origin: Germany

Temple-Anzani, 1923
Top speed: 121 mph (195 km/h)
Power: 116 cc
Country of origin: UK

Böhmerland, 1927
Top speed: 59 mph (95 km/h)
Power: 603 cc
Country of origin: Czech Republic

Ariel Square-Four, 1931
Top speed: 85 mph (137 km/h)
Power: 597 cc
Country of origin: UK

BMW Kompressor, 1935
Top speed: 130 mph (210 km/h)
Power: 492 cc
Country of origin: Germany

Indian Sports Scout, 1937
Top speed: 105 mph (169 km/h)
Power: 745 cc
Country of origin: US

Norton 500, 1938
Top speed: 110 mph (177 km/h)
Power: 490 cc
Country of origin: UK

Brough Superior Dream, 1938
Top speed: Not known
Power: 998 cc
Country of origin: UK

Vincent-HRD Series C Black Shadow, 1949
Top speed: 122 mph (196 km/h)
Power: 998 cc
Country of origin: UK

Zündapp KS601, 1950
Top speed: 87 mph (140 km/h)
Power: 597 cc
Country of origin: Germany

Indian Chief Roadmaster, 1950
Top speed: 85 mph (137 km/h)
Power: 1311 cc
Country of origin: US

Victoria Bergmeister, 1954
Top speed: 81 mph (130 km/h)
Power: 347 cc
Country of origin: Germany

Matchless G45, 1957
Top speed: 120 mph (193 km/h)
Power: 498 cc
Country of origin: UK

Gritzner Monza Super Sport, 1960
Top speed: 37 mph (60 km/h)
Power: 50 cc
Country of origin: Germany

Norton 650SS Dominator, 1962
Top speed: 115 mph (185 km/h)
Power: 646 cc
Country of origin: UK

Yamaha YDS3C Big Bear, 1965
Top speed: 88 mph (142 km/h)
Power: 246 cc
Country of origin: Japan

BSA Rocket 3, 1969
Top speed: 122 mph (196 km/h)
Power: 740 cc
Country of origin: UK

Triumph Trident Racer, 1971
Top speed: 164 mph (264 km/h)
Power: 749 cc
Country of origin: UK

Suzuki GT750, 1971
Top speed: 108 mph (174 km/hh)
Power: 738 cc
Country of origin: Japan

Honda Goldwing GL1500, 1975
Top speed: 116 mph (187 km/h)
Power: 1520 cc
Country of origin: Japan

Fantic Chopper, 1977
Top speed: 65 mph (105 km/h)
Power: 123 cc
Country of origin: Italy

Yamaha TZ250, 1979
Top speed: 140 mph (225 km/h)
Power: 247 cc
Country of origin: Japan

Laverda Jota, 1982
Top speed: 139 mph (224 km/h)
Power: 980 cc
Country of origin: Italy

BMW K1, 1983
Top speed: 125 mph (201 km/h)
Power: 988 cc
Country of origin: Germany

**Harley-Davidson
FLHX Electra Glide, 1984**
Top speed: 90 mph (145 km/h)
Power: 1312 cc
Country of origin: US

Aprilia RSV250, 1990
Top speed: 155 mph (250 km/h)
Power: 249 cc
Country of origin: Italy

Kawasaki ZZ-R1100, 1990
Top speed: 175 mph (282 km/h)
Power: 1052 cc
Country of origin: Japan

Honda XRV750, 1991
Top speed: 115 mph (185 km/h)
Power: 742 cc
Country of origin: Japan

Husqvarna TC610, 1992
Top speed: 90 mph (145 km/h)
Power: 577 cc
Country of origin: Sweden

Ducati M900 Monster, 1994
Top speed: 119 mph (192 km/h)
Power: 904 cc
Country of origin: Italy

Suzuki GSX1300R Hayabusa, 1999
Top speed: 186 mph (299 km/h)
Power: 1299 cc
Country of origin: Japan

Yamaha YZF1000 R1, 2001
Top speed: 165 mph (266 km/h)
Power: 998 cc
Country of origin: Japan

**Harley-Davidson
VRSCA V-ROD, 2003**
Top speed: 140 mph (225 km/h)
Power: 1130 cc
Country of origin: US

Easy rider

Harley-Davidson motorbikes, affectionately known as "Harleys" or "hogs", are big, heavy, and intended for long-distance, laid-back cruising. More than any other bikes, they are associated with alternative lifestyles and symbolize the freedom of the open road. Harleys look the part with classy chrome styling, and they sound it, too—their engines, usually air-cooled, produce a distinctive, deep rumble.

Legendary chopper
The Harley-Davidson Chopper was immortalized in the 1969 road movie *Easy Rider*, which followed the adventures of two dropout bikers. The Chopper's unique styling has very high handlebars and two different-sized wheels.

Feeling sporty
The Harley-Davidson Sportster has been in production since 1957—longer than any other Harley. Sportsters are the lightest and raciest Harley-Davidson bikes. The 1200 Sportster's top speed is 110 mph (177 km/h).

Need for speed
Staged on a straight, flat 0.25 mile (400-m) course, drag-racing events are all about hitting maximum speeds. The "trailer" on the back of the drag bike is a set of wheelie bars that prevent the front wheel from lifting too far off the ground when the bike is accelerating.

Born to be wild

Harley owners are passionate about their bikes and love to ride them in big groups. This rally took place outside Moscow, but the world's largest motorcycle event is the Harley-Davidson Love Ride rally, held in California each November. An association for Harley owners, the Harley Owners Group (HOG), was founded in 1983.

Sidecar action

A bike and a passenger sidecar are known as an "outfit." Harley-Davidson started making sidecars in 1914. In the 1920s, the company sold one sidecar for every two bikes. Harley-Davidson's Classic sidecar was produced between 1937 and 1966.

Law enforcement

Harley-Davidson sold its first police bike in 1908. The Harley's speed and maneuverability make it especially suitable for use by traffic police, but other law enforcers ride them, too. Today, more than 3,000 police departments across the USA use Harley-Davidsons.

HARLEY-DAVIDSON

William S. Harley and Arthur Davidson of Milwaukee, Wisconsin, sold their first motorcycle in 1903. By 1920, the Harley-Davidson Motor Company was the world's largest manufacturer of motorcycles. The famous bar-and-shield logo was patented as early as 1910, and the distinctive eagle design was added in 1933. Harley-Davidson motorcycles have been recognizable everywhere for their fine styling ever since.

Oldest	405 cc Single, debuted in 1903
Fastest	1994 VR1000, reaches top speeds of 190 mph (306 km/h)
Heaviest	1989 FLTC Tour-Glide, weighs a hefty 732 lbs (332kg)

VRSCA V-Rod

Launched in 2001, the VRSCA V-Rod was the most radically different Harley model in 50 years. Its liquid-cooled engine is extremely powerful and can take the bike to a top speed of 140 mph (225 km/h).

Speedometer

Dummy fuel tank

Engine

Tubular frame

Forks

Alloy wheel

Chrome muffler

Gearbox

Cooling radiator

Speedway

Racing motorbikes on oval dirt tracks first became popular in the 1920s. Speedway bikes are small and light, and they have no brakes, rear suspension, or gears. The races are usually between four riders, who score points depending on their performance over a set number of laps—three points for first place, two for second, one for third, and none for coming last. At the end of the heats, the rider with the most points is the champion. The biggest international tournament is the Fédération Internationale de Motorcyclisme (FIM) Speedway Grand Prix series.

Powersliding

Speedway tracks are covered in a sandy grit called shale. Although the bikes cannot brake as they enter a bend, the loose shale allows them to slide sideways—a technique known as powersliding. During the slide, the bike loses some speed through the back wheel, but keeps enough power to drive on around the bend.

Speedway facts

■ A speedway track must be between 855 ft (260 m) and 1,395 ft (425 m) long.

■ Longtrack is similar to speedway, but takes place on a 3,280-ft (1,000-m) track and is much faster.

■ Many speedway riders learn their skills on grasstrack racing, where they ride larger bikes on grass instead of shale circuits.

■ The first ever speedway races took place in Australia in 1923. They were organized by New Zealander Johnny Hoskins.

■ A klaxon horn or a bell sounds a two-minute warning before each heat, so that the riders can prepare to race.

■ The heat winner is the rider whose front wheel passes over the finish line first, after completing all the laps (usually four).

Around the circuit

The countries where speedway is most popular are Poland, Sweden, Denmark, and the UK. Speedway meetings attract large crowds. A speedway meeting may have more than 20 heats, but each heat is over in less than a minute.

Speedway sidecar racing

Ordinary sidecars are attached to the side of a motorbike to carry a passenger. Sidecars built for speedway are an integral part of the machine. The sidecars are low to the ground and whip up tremendous plumes of dust as they zoom around the dirt track.

Ice racing

One of the strangest kinds of motorcycle racing is ice racing. The riders speed their brakeless bikes around an ice-covered stadium track. They accelerate to 81 mph (130 km/h) on the straights, lean through the turns, and angle for the inside position. Ice racing began in Germany in 1925. The earliest races took place on frozen lakes.

Throttle

Fuel tank

Front suspension damper

Mudguard

Rear-wheel disk

Rear-wheel dirt deflector

Single cylinder four-stroke engine

The front tire has a maximum width of 4 in (100 mm).

Serious spikes

For better traction on the frozen track, ice-racing bike tires are studded with hundreds of screws or spikes, some as long as 2.5 in (6.5 cm). The bikes have two-speed gearboxes, too. Riders still take plenty of tumbles, so they wear safety helmets and thick, padded leather suits to protect themselves.

Built for speed

A speedway bike has about the same accelerating power as a Formula One racing car. It has a 30.5 cu in (500 cc) single-cylinder four-stroke engine that runs on pure methanol (racing alcohol), rather than gasoline, for safety reasons—methanol is less likely to explode in the event of a crash.

headlight

Top yoke and handlebar mounting

Cable from alternator to lights

Gear-change lever

Left-h footr

Carbon-fiber front mudguard

Oil cooler

Tubular st trellis fram

Upper section of airbox

Front fork suspension

1000 S ds

Right-hand plastic bodywork

Air filter

Front wheel

Lower section of airbox

Fuel injection bodies

Front tire

Drive chain

Front sprocket

Building the bike

The Ducati Multistrada 1000S DS is designed specifically to combine sporty performance with the comforts of a touring motorcyle, and its components reflect this. The chassis, or frame, is made of tubular steel, which is welded into triangular sections that make it extremely strong. This is covered with tough but lightweight carbon-fiber body parts, such as the front mudguard, and comfort-oriented components like the padded seat, raised handlebars, and remote-controlled headlight adjuster.

Signal light on front of rearview mirror

Rearview mirror

Front brake lever

Throttle cables

Throttle

Ignition lock

Key

Light switch and cable

Aluminum handlebars

Speedometer

Plastic nose cone

Upper fairing and screen

Brake calipers

Plastic air circulation panel

DUCATI

Main

Road racer

The sporty Multistrada 1000S DS motorcycle is produced by Italian motorbike manufacturer, Ducati. The bike's name, "Multistrada," means "many road," and it is designed to be ridden on all types of road surface, from city streets to highways. The result is a bike that is fast and nimble but is still comfortable. There is even an extra seat so a passenger can jump on, hold onto the grab rail, and enjoy the experience of a thrilling ride!

Racing red

The color of Ducati's bikes is limited to a small palette. This Multistrada also comes in black, and some models are available in yellow, but Ducati red remains the manufacturer's most famous color. Why red? In the early days of international racing, red was the color chosen by Italian competitors, just as "racing green" was the choice of the English entrants.

DUCATI

1000 S DS

Comfort and safety

The single rear shock absorber is adjustable, which allows the rider to sit higher or lower. The drilled disk brakes at the center of the wheels help to improve braking consistency. In wet weather, the drill-holes prevent a film of water from forming over the disks.

FRONT VIEW

REAR VIEW

Head protection
Early helmets were made of soft materials that simply cushioned the rider's head. Modern helmets incorporate layered materials, including plastic, so they provide more effective protection.

Safety gear
The correct clothing is essential for a motorcyclist's safety. As bikes have become faster, specialist body armor made mainly from leather has been developed. The leather is treated to ensure suppleness and absorb impact.

Performance rubber
The engine's power goes to the rear wheel, and the extra width of the rear tire provides added stability. Both front and rear tires are grooved for use on the road. They are made from a "sticky" rubber that enables them to grip the road surface.

Rear view of
exhaust muffler

Exhaust
muffler

Bracket and
screws for
exhaust system

Padded
passenger's
seat

Clutch lever

Front cylinder exhaust pipe

Exhaust header
pipes

Exhaust pipe from
catalytic converter
to muffler

Padded
rider's seat

Light switch
and cable

Plastic tail

Exhaust
gasket

Clutch operating
cylinder

Side profile of
main bodywork

Passenger
grab rail

Catalytic
converter

Steel plate to attach
exhaust muffler to frame

Fuel cap

Italian license plate

Rear light
cluster

Combined tank/seat unit

Engine casing

I CC ® BO
158/9

Brake lever

Right-hand footrest

Stand

Crankshaft

Drive gears

Bottom cylinder

Clutch basket

Clutch gears

Clutch pressure plate

Inner-toothed clutch plates (9)

Outer-toothed clutch plates (7)

Clutch casing

Flywheel

Left-hand plastic bodywork and glove compartment

1000 S DS

Camshaft drive belts

Drive belt cover

Alternator

Top cylinder

Alternator cover

Rear shock absorber

Gear selector drum

Starter motor

Battery

DUCATI YUASA MF YT12B-BS

Gear cluster

Tie rod for transferring suspension movement

Gear selector mechanism

Rear sprocket

Sensor to link alternator to electrical parts

Clip, nut, and washer

Rear wheel

Rear tire

Swingarm

High rollers
The world's longest convoy of Rolls-Royces was on May 20, 2000, when 420 cars drove for two miles (3.2 km) along the A55 near Chester, UK.

Longest limousine
The world's longest car is a 100-ft (30.5-m) limousine built in California. It has six wheels, a swimming pool, and a king-size waterbed.

Biggest bus fleet
The Andhra Pradesh State Road Transport Company in southern India runs more than 18,300 buses.

Longest train ride
The world's longest single train ride is on the Trans-Siberian Railroad. The journey takes eight days and crosses 6,346 miles (10,214 km) from Moscow, Russia, to Pyongyang, North Korea.

Fastest cyclist
The fastest bicycle speed is 167 mph (268.8 km/h), achieved by Dutch cyclist Fred Rompelberg at Bonneville Salt Flats, Utah, on October 3, 1995.

Most popular car
Toyota Corollas were first produced in 1966. Since then, more than 25 million Toyota Corollas have been made worldwide.

Most subway stops
The MTA subway system in New York City has the most subway stops, with 468 stations in a network of 230 miles (370 km).

Longest freight train

The record for the largest freight train is 4.6 miles (7.4 km) long. It consisted of 682 cars and was assembled by Australia's BHP mining company in 2001.

Longest journey on a motorbike

Between January 1985 and April 1995, Emilio Scotto of Argentina rode the world's longest motorcycle journey, crossing 457,000 miles (735,000 km) and 214 countries.

Busiest railroad

The East Japan Railroad Company is the world's busiest railroad. Every day, the railroad carries around 16 million passengers in the eastern parts of Japan, including the city of Tokyo.

Best-selling vehicle

Since 1958, the Honda Motor Company has sold more than 50 million Honda Super Cub motorcycles, making it the most popular vehicle ever.

Highest monster truck jump

"Bigfoot" made the world's highest monster truck jump, soaring 24 ft (7.3 meters) in Las Vegas on December 14, 1999.

Longest road train

On February 18, 2006, the world's longest road train hauled 113 trailers measuring 4,836.9 ft (1,474.3 m) on its short journey in Queensland, Australia.

Land record

As people strive for land transportation to be bigger, better, more powerful, and more efficient, the record books are bursting with land-lubbing firsts. New records are made and old records are broken, from the busiest railroads to the longest motorcycle journeys. There are also marvels of engineering, including the construction of a freight train that was 682 cars long, and the most outlandish of stretch limousines that has its own swimming pool!

Most people to fit in a Mini

On July 3, 2000, a record-breaking 18 people crammed into a Mini Cooper car in Birmingham, UK.

Air

Timeline

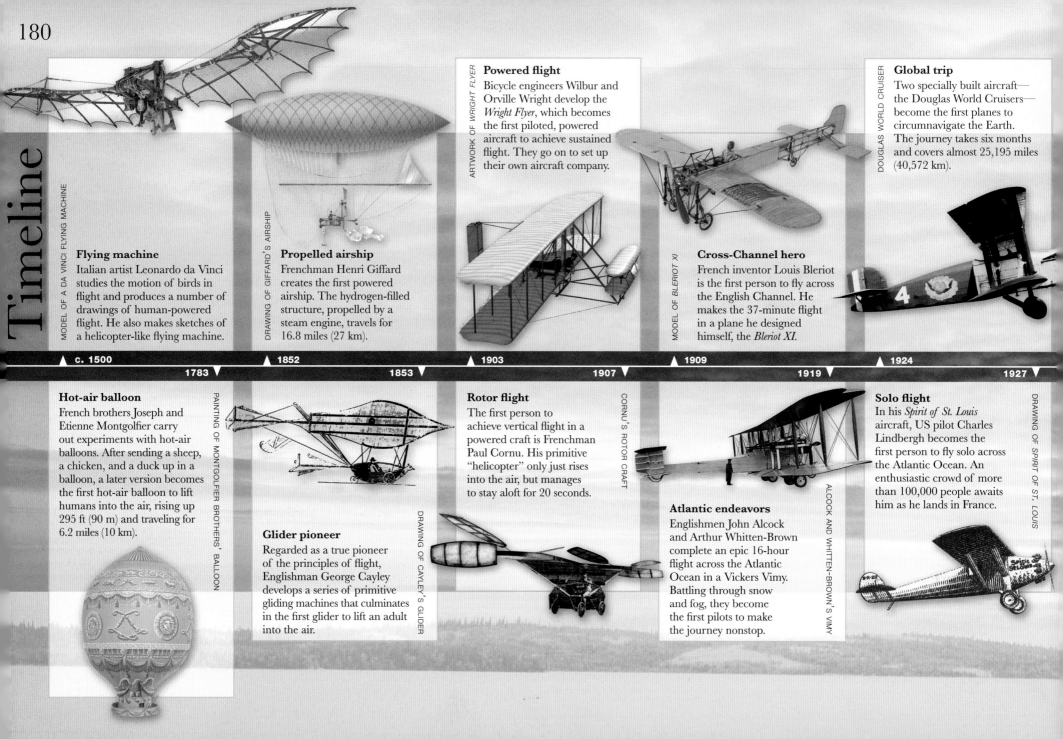

Flying machine
Italian artist Leonardo da Vinci studies the motion of birds in flight and produces a number of drawings of human-powered flight. He also makes sketches of a helicopter-like flying machine.

MODEL OF A DA VINCI FLYING MACHINE

Propelled airship
Frenchman Henri Giffard creates the first powered airship. The hydrogen-filled structure, propelled by a steam engine, travels for 16.8 miles (27 km).

DRAWING OF GIFFARD'S AIRSHIP

Powered flight
Bicycle engineers Wilbur and Orville Wright develop the *Wright Flyer*, which becomes the first piloted, powered aircraft to achieve sustained flight. They go on to set up their own aircraft company.

ARTWORK OF *WRIGHT FLYER*

Cross-Channel hero
French inventor Louis Bleriot is the first person to fly across the English Channel. He makes the 37-minute flight in a plane he designed himself, the *Bleriot XI*.

MODEL OF *BLERIOT XI*

Global trip
Two specially built aircraft— the Douglas World Cruisers— become the first planes to circumnavigate the Earth. The journey takes six months and covers almost 25,195 miles (40,572 km).

DOUGLAS WORLD CRUISER

▲ c. 1500   ▲ 1852   ▲ 1903   ▲ 1909   ▲ 1924

1783 ▼   1853 ▼   1907 ▼   1919 ▼   1927 ▼

Hot-air balloon
French brothers Joseph and Etienne Montgolfier carry out experiments with hot-air balloons. After sending a sheep, a chicken, and a duck up in a balloon, a later version becomes the first hot-air balloon to lift humans into the air, rising up 295 ft (90 m) and traveling for 6.2 miles (10 km).

PAINTING OF MONTGOLFIER BROTHERS' BALLOON

Glider pioneer
Regarded as a true pioneer of the principles of flight, Englishman George Cayley develops a series of primitive gliding machines that culminates in the first glider to lift an adult into the air.

DRAWING OF CAYLEY'S GLIDER

Rotor flight
The first person to achieve vertical flight in a powered craft is Frenchman Paul Cornu. His primitive "helicopter" only just rises into the air, but manages to stay aloft for 20 seconds.

CORNU'S ROTOR CRAFT

Atlantic endeavors
Englishmen John Alcock and Arthur Whitten-Brown complete an epic 16-hour flight across the Atlantic Ocean in a Vickers Vimy. Battling through snow and fog, they become the first pilots to make the journey nonstop.

ALCOCK AND WHITTEN-BROWN'S VIMY

Solo flight
In his *Spirit of St. Louis* aircraft, US pilot Charles Lindbergh becomes the first person to fly solo across the Atlantic Ocean. An enthusiastic crowd of more than 100,000 people awaits him as he lands in France.

DRAWING OF *SPIRIT OF ST. LOUIS*

Passenger airliner
The De Havilland DH106 Comet takes off for the first time. It is designed to be the world's first commercial jet airliner, and becomes fully operational after three more years of testing. It can carry more passengers faster around the world than any previous aircraft.

DE HAVILLAND DH106 COMET

Jet-powered flight
The German Heinkel He 178, the world's first jet-powered aircraft, makes its maiden flight. It has short wooden wings and can fly at speeds in excess of 400 mph (644 km/h).

HENKEL HE 178

Supersonic flight
The prototype of the Russian Tupolev Tu-144 takes to the skies. It becomes the first commercial airliner to travel at Mach 2 (twice the speed of sound).

TUPOLEV TU-144

Atlantic crossing
Piloted by Ben Abruzzo, Maxie Anderson, and Larry Newman, *Double Eagle II* becomes the first balloon to fly across the Atlantic Ocean. After setting off from Maine, the balloon lands in a field north of Paris, France, almost six days later.

DOUBLE EAGLE II

Balloon adventure
Bertrand Piccard from Switzerland and Briton Brian Jones complete the first circumnavigation of the world in a balloon. Their *Breitling Orbiter 3* takes just under 20 days to make the trip.

BREITLING ORBITER 3

1939   1947   1949   1961   1968   1969   1978   1981   1999   2005

Breaking the sound barrier
US test pilot Charles "Chuck" Yeager becomes the fastest man on Earth when his Bell X-1 rocket-powered aircraft exceeds the speed of sound while flying at 43,027 ft (13,110 m) over the Mojave Desert in California.

BELL X-1

Human in space
Russian cosmonaut Yuri Gagarin is the first person to orbit Earth. At the end of his 108-minute flight in *Vostok I*, he ejects from the craft and parachutes safely down to Earth.

YURI GAGARIN

Moon landing
American Neil Armstrong lands the *Eagle* lunar module on the Moon. Armstrong and fellow astronaut Buzz Aldrin become the first people to walk on the surface of the Moon.

NEIL ARMSTRONG'S PHOTO OF BUZZ ALDRIN

Reusable spacecraft
Exactly 20 years to the day after Yuri Gagarin's debut space flight, the world's first reusable spacecraft, the Space Shuttle *Columbia*, embarks on its maiden mission. After orbiting Earth for about 55 hours, *Columbia* lands on a runway in California, USA.

SPACE SHUTTLE COLUMBIA

Mammoth aircraft
The world's biggest passenger airliner, the Airbus A380, makes its maiden flight from Toulouse, France. Once operational, it will be able to carry more than 850 passengers.

AIRBUS A380

- There is evidence of basic hot-air balloons being used for military signaling in Ancient China.

- Joseph and Jacques Montgolfier developed the first passenger balloon in 1783.

- In 1709, Bartolemeu de Gusmao made the first working model of a hot-air balloon in Portugal.

- Hot-air balloons were used as lookout posts in the American Civil War of 1861–65.

- The first passengers in the Montgolfier balloon were a duck, a sheep, and a chicken.

- The longest time spent in a balloon was 477 hours, 47 minutes— a record set in 1999.

- Balloons do not fly in the rain because water heated by the balloon can damage the fabric.

- The highest altitude attained by a manned balloon was 64,997 ft (19,811 m) by Per Lindstrand in 1988.

- Weather balloons can record data from up to 25 miles (40 km) high in the atmosphere.

- Balloon baskets are woven from sturdy Kooboo and Palambang cane.

- Every hot-air balloon pilot must keep a record of his or her flights in a log book.

- Modern hot-air balloons use propane gas in the burner to heat the air.

- In 1978, the helium-filled *Double Eagle II* was the first balloon to cross the Atlantic.

- The world's largest ever balloon was the *Virgin Pacific Flyer*. It had a volume of 2,613,000 cu ft (74,000 cu m).

- The first hot-air balloon to traverse the Pacific was crewed by Richard Branson and Per Lindstrand in 1991.

- The actual balloon structure is called the envelope—it is made of long, nylon sections called gores.

Hot air

The oldest human flight technology, hot-air balloons can be made into almost any shape, although the upside-down teardrop is the most common. Passengers are carried in a lightweight wicker basket. Liquid gas in cylinders positioned at the base of the balloon heats the air in the balloon, and this makes it rise up. The balloonist maneuvers the balloon by climbing to different wind currents at different altitudes. When it is time to descend, hot air is slowly released.

- The bottom part of the envelope is called the skirt and is made of a flame-resistant material.

- For most nylon envelopes, the maximum internal temperature is limited to about 248°F (120°C).

- Balloon pilots need a specialist ballon pilot's license to fly a balloon.

- An airship differs from a balloon in that it can be propelled through the air.

- The world's largest balloon manufacturer is Cameron Balloons, based in England. It makes about 500 a year.

- A hot-air balloon pilot travels horizontally by flying with different air.

- Preflight, pilots sometimes release a helium-filled balloon to check the wind direction.

- The biggest hot-air balloons are able to carry 20 passengers.

- A ground crew follows a balloon and picks up its passengers when it lands.

- Instruments on a hot-air balloon include an altimeter to monitor the balloon's height, and a variometer to show the speed it is rising or falling.

- Before a balloon is fully inflated, it is often attached to a vehicle on the ground.

- The fastest circumnavigation of the world in a balloon was 320 hours, 33 minutes by Spirit of Freedom in 2002.

- Hot-air balloons are almost silent, so they are an ideal way of observing wildlife on a safari.

- In 1999, the Breitling Orbiter 3 made the first successful around-the-world trip in a balloon.

- The largest balloon festival in the world is the annual Albuquerque International Balloon Fiesta, where up to 750 balloons are flown.

Airships

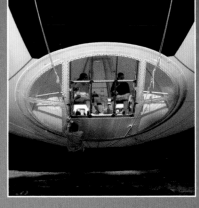

Zeppelin NT
A modern version of the legendary German Zeppelin company has developed an airship called the NT ("New Technology"). Designed for advertising and research purposes, it first flew in September 1997.

While the airships of today are more advanced than those that flew in the "golden age" of airships in the 1920s and 1930s, the principles of this type of flight remain exactly the same. Essentially, a container holds a gas that is lighter than the air outside of it, thereby raising it into the sky. This can be achieved either by inserting the gas—usually helium—into a framework covered with fabric, or simply by filling the material with gas and expanding it.

Takeoff and landing
When the Zeppelin takes off, its nose cone is detached from the mast truck. It lands by being maneuvered into position alongside the mast and a cable is then attached to the nose. The cable is tightened and the Zeppelin is locked in place. A ground crew of just three people is required.

Futuristic design
This Canadian airship has been created using the latest technology. Its unique spherical design—it is shaped like a football—has no stabilizing fins, and the crew actually sit within the structure rather than in an external cabin. In 2003, it set a manned airship altitude world record when it flew up to 20,453 ft (6,234 m). An attempt at an around-the-world flight is planned for the future.

Blimps
Nonrigid airships have no frame inside them and are commonly known as blimps. Some are used as gantries for TV cameras to capture overhead shots at sports events or for research purposes. Others operate simply as high-level advertising boards in the sky.

ZEPPELIN NT

Built in Friedrichshafen, Germany, the Zeppelin NT is used for various commercial missions and also operates tourist flights over Lake Constance. The cabin comfortably seats 12 passengers and includes a food galley and toilet facilities.

Specifications

Length: 246 ft (75 m)	
Width: 64 ft (19.5 m)	
Height: 57 ft (17.4 m)	
Balloon capacity: 290,474 cu ft (8,225 cu m) of nonflammable helium	
Passengers: 12	
Range: 559 miles (900 km)	
Top speed: 78 mph (125 km/h)	
Maximum time in air without having to descend: 24 hours	

Airship trivia

■ The world's biggest airships were the *Hindenburg* and *Graf Zeppelin II*. Built in the 1930s, they measured 804 ft (245 m) in length and could travel at speeds up to 84 mph (135 km/h).

■ Luxury airships from the 1920s included grand lounges, dining rooms, kitchens, passenger cabins, crew quarters, and observation decks.

■ A US company plans to build an airship similar in size to the airships of the 1930s, which will be able to carry 250 passengers nonstop for 6,000 miles (9,660 km).

■ High-altitude airships are being developed for use as telecommunication centres in the outer-atmosphere where bad weather cannot affect the signals.

■ Other designs for future airships include one for transporting cargo and another to fight forest fires.

The propellers can be tilted up or down.

A multilayer fabric covers the airship's rigid framework.

The side propeller steers the airship on its chosen course.

The casing hides one of three engines.

The rear propeller pushes the airship through the air.

Free fall

Skydivers leap from planes and hurtle toward the ground at speeds of 125 mph (200 km/h) or more. This is called free fall, where nothing slows their descent until they pull the rip cord and their parachutes open. Some skydivers perform set moves in a form of aerial gymnastics, while others use a skyboard to surf through the air with no force acting on the body except gravity. Bungee jumping is another activity that appeals to free-fall addicts, while hang-gliding offers a longer-lasting experience in the air.

Leap of faith
Once the plane door opens, the skydivers jump out one by one. First-timers usually dive from around 3,000 ft (914 m), which gives three seconds of free fall. The more adventurous dive from 10,990 ft (3,350 m) and enjoy 45 seconds of free fall. Experienced divers jump from even higher altitudes.

Air waves
With feet strapped to a skyboard, a skysurfer surfs, slides, spins, and twists in free fall. The display lasts about a minute, before the parachute is deployed. It is recorded on film by the surfer's cojumper, who is known as the cameraflyer.

Piled high

For some skydivers, the acrobatics do not begin until their parachutes have been deployed. Parachute formation skydivers wear specially constructed parachutes that can be joined together in the air to form stacks or other shapes.

Precision landing

Parachute landing is a skill that involves aiming for a spot and reaching it with the body in the right position. There is a competitive skydiving category called "accuracy landing," where the skydiver tries to land on a 1.25-in (3-cm) target.

Elastic leap

With just an elastic harness attached to the torso or leg, bungee jumpers leap from cliffs, bridges, and buildings. Regulars master a variety of jump styles. A water touchdown involves dipping into water at the bottom.

Flying formations

Nicknamed "belly flying," formation skydiving is when teams of skydivers link up in the air and perform aerobatic displays. Competitive formation flying is done in teams of 4, 8, or 16. Recreational skydivers often jump in much larger groups, just for fun!

Hanging around

A glider is an unpowered aircraft. The hang-glider pilot hangs in a harness from the wing and uses a metal bar to control the glider and make the best use of air currents. Some pilots launch themselves off cliffs, while others are towed into the air by small, engine-powered planes.

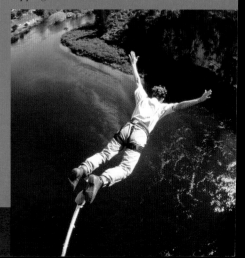

Largest formation: 400 people (Thailand, 2006)   **Most people on a bungee rope:** 31 (Germany, 2000)   **Highest bungee jump from a building:** 590 ft 10 in (180.1 m) (New Zealand, 1998)

Huge helicopter

The world's biggest helicopter is the Russian Mil Mi-26. It is used by the air force to transport troops and heavy equipment. Also used by the United Nations, the Mi-26 is able to carry 63 passengers or 20 tons of cargo.

Rotor power

Microlight

The smallest form of rotor-powered flight is the microlight, or ultralight. It consists of a basic frame containing one or two seats, with an engine behind it and rotor blades above it. Most microlights fly at speeds less than 62 mph (100 km/h).

Helicopters, gyrocopters, and other types of rotor-powered aircraft are different from fixed-wing planes because they can hover, take off vertically, and fly backward. It makes them more maneuverable than fixed-wing aircraft and means they can land in far more difficult terrain. This is why helicopters are the ideal form of transportation for military air forces and for humanitarian missions, such as reaching remote areas affected by natural disasters.

Fast flier

Known as a slowed-rotor compound aircraft, the prototype CarterCopter uses a rotor to takeoff vertically like a helicopter, and a wing so it can fly at speeds of up to 500 mph (805 km/h). However, it is not able to hover.

Clockwise chopper

One of the world's biggest helicopter makers, Eurocopter produces a range that includes the EC120. The rotor blades on Eurocopter craft turn clockwise, which is the opposite to all US-made craft, though the effect is exactly the same.

Rotor facts

■ In 1480, Italian artist and inventor Leonardo da Vinci sketched an idea for a craft that would spin as it moved through the air. His "helical air screw" was one of the first drawings of a helicopter ever.

■ Ukrainian Igor Sikorsky developed what would be the first fully operational rotary-bladed helicopter in 1939. He later founded a successful helicopter manufacturing company that carried his name.

■ As well as being the world's largest helicopter, the Mil Mi-26 was also the first helicopter to use eight rotor blades.

■ Unlike a fixed-wing aircraft pilot, a helicopter pilot needs to use both arms and legs at the same time to fly the craft.

■ Tandem rotor helicopters, such as the US Chinook, have two main sets of rotor blades and no tail rotor.

■ Helicopters are used by a variety of professions, including the police, air ambulance services, and farmers.

■ There are more than 15,000 civilian helicopters in operation around the world.

Cockpit controls

A helicopter pilot needs to control three things at the same time. The first is the collective control stick, which lifts or lowers the craft. The second is the cyclic control stick, which moves the helicopter forward, backward, and sideways. The third is the foot pedals, which control the angle of the tail rotor.

Rotor safety

Eurocopter developed the enclosed tail rotor, which features on all of its helicopters. Also known as a "fenestron," it is considered to be safer than traditional exposed rotor designs and is also more fuel-efficient.

1 The nose is one of a number of sections assembled in the "low hangar" area of the main building. Inner frame sections are put together and outer body panels are then fixed on to them. These sections are joined together to make the shell of the cockpit and nose.

Plane production

Building a luxury personal jet such as the Gulfstream G550 is a high-tech process. At the company's plant in Savannah, the different elements of the plane, such as the fuselage, nose, and wings, are assembled separately before being joined together. It is a super-efficient assembly line—as soon as one section is finished, it moves along to the next team until, just 18 weeks later, the complete aircraft is ready to be tested and fitted out.

1 The fuselage is made up of three sections—forward, center, and aft. These start off as flat panels and a machine bends them into a curved shape. They are then secured tightly, ready to be worked on.

3 After internal ribs have been added, three upper parts of the forward fuselage section are joined together. At the same time, other teams construct the center and aft sections, nose, and tail.

4 The three fuselage sections are moved to the "high hangar" area of the building. Here, they are all joined to form one fuselage. The completed nose section is also added at this stage.

5 The wing sections arrive at the plant by rail and are joined together in the largest part of the main building. They are then attached to the fuselage. The finished tail section is also attached to the aircraft.

6 The engines are delivered to Gulfstream in kit form. They are suspended in the air and then assembled. Once checked, the completed engine units are attached to the fuselage.

7 The aircraft is moved to a test hangar. This is where everything apart from the engines and the auxilliary power unit is checked, including the plane's complex electronic systems.

8 After testing the engines, the aircraft is flown and given its certificate of airworthiness. Finally, it is moved to the "completion center" where it is painted and fitted out before being delivered to the buyer.

War birds

Military aircraft are the most advanced flying machines in the world. Aside from spacecraft and rockets, they can travel faster and higher than anything else in the sky. Some incorporate "stealth" technology, which uses special construction materials and electronics to enable the aircraft to go undetected by other planes in the sky and radar on the ground. Pilots of jet fighters, bombers, and reconnaissance planes need to react quickly to cope with flying at up to three times the speed of sound. They are assisted by sophisticated computer displays that identify and track potential threats, and provide navigation information.

Angled fin blocks heat from the engine exhaust to prevent radar detection.

Clipped delta (triangular) wing is made of strong, lightweight titanium.

Engines generate more thrust than any other fighter aircraft.

Leading edge of horizontal stabilizer is at the same angle as front of wing.

Each of the two weapons bays houses three missiles or a bomb.

The radar system is housed in Raptor's nose.

The inlet spike can be moved inward to allow more air into the engine, which prevents damage from the shockwave produced when the plane breaks the speed of sound.

F-22A RAPTOR

The world's newest and most sophisticated supersonic fighter is the American F-22A Raptor. It combines stealth technology with exceptional thrust to create an aircraft that can fly virtually undetected at almost twice the speed of sound. The Raptor's powerful engines allow it to fly in "supercruise" mode. This means it does not need to waste fuel by using an afterburner to provide additional thrust.

Specifications	
Length	62 ft (18.9 m)
Wingspan	44 ft 6 in (13.6 m)
Wing area	840 sq ft (78 sq m)
Engine thrust	70,000 lb (31,760 kg)
Range	2,000 miles (3,220 km)
Top speed	1,500 mph+ (2,413.5 km/h+)
Maximum altitude	50,000 ft+ (15,235 m+)

SR-71 BLACKBIRD

The Lockheed SR-71 Blackbird was one of the earliest aircraft to be designed to avoid radar detection. It first flew in 1964 and was so fast that if pilots detected a surface-to-air missile, they would simply accelerate to evade it. The Blackbird was the world's fastest operational aircraft until it was retired in 1998. It still holds the New York to London flight time record of 1 hour 55 minutes.

Specifications	
Length	107 ft 5 in (16.94 m)
Wingspan	55 ft 6 in (29.480 m)
Wing area	3,680 sq ft (170 sq m)
Engine thrust	65,000 lb (29,480 kg)
Range	1,830 miles (5,926 km)
Top speed	2,193 mph (3,528.5 km/h)
Maximum altitude	85,000 ft (25,910 m)

There are two cockpits, one for the pilot (front) and another for the reconnaissance systems operator (rear).

The Pratt & Whitney engine is one of the most powerful in the world.

Special deep-blue paint contains tiny iron balls that help reflect radar-seeking radiation waves.

The airframe is made of titanium alloy to withstand the intense heat generated when traveling at high speed.

Nose probe measures the plane's speed.

Air intake for one of the four engines

The cockpit accommodates pilot and commander.

Electronic sensors

The wing design creates minimal drag and helps avoid radar detection.

B-2 SPIRIT

The Northrop B-2 Spirit first flew in 1989. It was developed to fly long-range missions while avoiding enemy radar detection. Its unique "flying wing" shape is just one of its stealth characteristics, adding to the aircraft's "invisibility." It can carry 40,000 lb (18,144 kg) of weapons and fly 6,905 miles (11,112 km) without refueling.

Specifications	
Length	69 ft (21 m)
Wingspan	172 ft (52.46 m)
Wing area	5,000 sq ft (465 sq m)
Engine thrust	69,199 lb (31,388 kg)
Range	6,905 miles (11,112 km)
Top speed	528 mph (850 km/h)
Maximum altitude	50,000 ft (15,240 m)

At the controls

The flight deck of a modern airliner contains an array of visual displays, levers, and switches. The cockpit of this Airbus A330 also incorporates innovative side control-sticks that enable the pilot to bank, climb, or descend the plane. Pilots receive regular training to ensure that they fully understand the function of every lever and button.

Cockpit facts

■ Navigating a modern airliner involves using radio waves to plot route markers, although an increasing number of planes use GPS (Global Positioning System) to guide them.

■ In a traditional cockpit, there is one control column for the pilot and another for the copilot, so either can fly the plane.

■ Some airlines allow passengers to visit an aircraft's cockpit before or after—but never during—a flight.

■ Although an autopilot system can be used to fly a plane and land it, takeoffs are always carried out manually.

■ The pilot operates a mini steering wheel to direct the aircraft's nosewheel when it is taxiing on the ground.

■ Some planes can fly for up to three hours on one engine if the second one fails.

1. The **Primary Flight Display** shows vital information such as air speed, banking, and barometric pressure.

2. The **Navigation Display** shows the aircraft's position and course, which is plotted by an internal computer.

3. Switches on the **Flight Control Unit** engage and disengage the autopilot, and also control speed.

4. Engine data processed by a centralized monitor shows up on the **Primary Engine Display**.

5. Additional engine information, including fuel use, is presented on the **Secondary Engine Display**.

6. The **Multipurpose Control and Display Unit (MCDU)** displays the flight management system.

7. The **Switching Panel** checks that the aircraft is configured correctly for takeoff.

8. The **Thrust Control System** sets the engines to reverse idle, forward idle, climb, thrust, or takeoff power.

9. Controls for radio communications and frequency selection are on the **Radio Management Panel**.

10. The **Audio Controls** contain radio and public announcement transmission panels and switches.

11. Switches in the **Lighting Controls** operate the lighting systems in the aircraft's passenger cabin.

12. The **Flap Lever** commands the positions of the flaps and wing slats during takeoff and landing.

Computerized controls

The A330 uses the same fly-by-wire computer technology first pioneered by Airbus on its A320 in 1988. This allows a pilot to input flight data into a central processing unit, which then controls the operation of the aircraft—essentially, the plane is able to fly by itself. It results in a safer form of flying because the onboard computers cannot exceed the predetermined limits set by the pilot.

(13) The **Trim Selector** sets the rudder's neutral position and indicates the direction and extent of rudder trim.

(14) Air brakes or wing spoilers to slow the aircraft for landing are operated by the **Speed Brake Lever**.

(15) Fly-by-wire systems are controlled by the **Side Stick**, and are activated by pressing the red button.

(16) For steering on the ground, the aircraft's nose wheel is turned by the **Nose Wheel Steering Tiller**.

(17) The **Rudder Pedal** is a foot control used to turn the rudder and swing the tail to the left or right.

(18) Situated between rudder pedals, the **Foot Rest** is used by the pilot while the plane is in autopilot mode.

(19) The **Overhead Control Panel** houses emergency and oxygen systems, and a voice recorder.

(20) A working **Tray Table** slides out from underneath the instrument panel over the pilot's lap.

(21) Traditional "needle-and-dial" **Analog Instruments** are used if the computer displays fail.

(22) The **Captain's Seat** is always the left seat on a flight deck, and it slides back on tracks for access.

(23) The **First Officer's Seat** is always the right seat on a flight deck, with duplicate controls and instruments.

(24) If either of the two primary MCDUs fail, the **Backup Multipurpose Control and Display Unit** is used.

Sky life

Each year, millions of people travel on passenger jets such as this Boeing 747. Soaring above the clouds at speeds of 567 mph (912 km/h), the largest versions of these aircraft can carry more than 500 passengers and crew.

Airline pilots and co-pilots never get the same in-flight meal in case of food poisoning.

Laptops and CD players are banned during takeoff and landing because they emit electromagnetic radiation that could interfere with the plane's navigation equipment.

Most airlines no longer serve peanuts on flights because of the risk to people with nut allergies.

Airplanes have vacuum toilets. When one is flushed, a valve opens on the sewer line and the vacuum in the line sucks the contents of the bowl into a tank.

The 747 is made up of more than 6 million parts—half of which are fasteners such as bolts.

The 747's windshield contains special glass to help filter the glare of the Sun. The flight deck crew also wears sunglasses.

Pilots have to be clean-shaven—a beard could stop the oxygen mask from fitting tightly enough if the cabin pressure dropped suddenly.

There is no standard seat size so each airline can decide its own dimensions. Generally, seats are bigger and there is more legroom in first class and business class than in economy class.

The number of flight attendants on a 747 flight is determined by the number of emergency exits. The biggest 747s have 12 emergency exits, so they have a minimum of 12 attendants.

The senior flight attendant is responsible for carrying diplomatic mail from country to country. There is a lockup to keep the documents safe.

If the power fails in an emergency, special batteries supply electricity to emergency lights, pilot radios, and the passenger address (PA) system.

More than 4.3 miles (7 km) of wiring is needed to run the in-flight entertainment system on the plane.

For each flight, catering crews prepare, cook, and chill 5 tons of food and beverage. The food is prepared in bulk on the ground, chilled, then reheated on the plane.

Three billion meals are consumed on planes every year.

Our taste buds are less able to distinguish flavours in food and drink at high altitudes, which could help explain the bad reputation of airline food.

Air is supplied to the cabin through the engines. It is passed through air-conditioning units, where it is cooled before being pumped into the cabin.

It is important for passengers on long flights to move about the cabin regularly to avoid getting cramps or blood clots.

Microwave ovens cannot be used on planes since they would interfere with the radar systems. The food is reheated in ovens in the galleys and then distributed by flight attendants.

During a typical international flight, more than 50,000 in-flight service items, such as cutlery, are used.

As the aircraft ascends, the change in pressure can cause your ears to hurt and then "pop" as they return to normal.

The 747 fleet has flown 3.6 billion people—the equivalent of more than half the world's population.

Airplanes fly at high altitudes where the air is thin, so cabins are pressurized to ensure that the air pressure is almost the same as at sea level.

There are eight bunks at the back of the plane and two bunks on the flight deck for the crew to use when resting.

Giant in the sky

The Airbus A380 is the largest passenger airliner in the world, capable of carrying more than 850 people. The parts that make up the aircraft are produced at locations all over the globe. They are then transported by land, sea, and air to the main A380 plant at Toulouse, in France. Here, the giant double-decker aircraft is assembled and tested before being flown to Hamburg, Germany, to be fitted out and painted in the airlines' brand colors.

By sea

A specially built ship transports sections of the plane's fuselage from Hamburg, Germany, to Mostyn in Wales, where the A380's wings are collected. The ship then travels to St. Nazaire in France. Here, more fuselage sections are loaded on before the ship sails to its final destination near Bordeaux, in France.

By air

Vertical tailplane sections for the A380 are manufactured in Stade, Germany. From there, the 46.3-ft- (14.1-m-) tall tails are loaded onto an Airbus Beluga transporter aircraft and flown to Toulouse, in France.

By road

After the ship has docked near Bordeaux, the fuselage, wings, and tailplane parts are loaded onto barges. These travel down to Langon, also in France, where the A380 parts are unloaded and placed on specially adapted trailers for the road journey to Toulouse. To minimize disruption, the trucks travel only at night.

First in line

In May 2004, the first A380 came off the final assembly line in Toulouse. It was then moved to another hangar where it began its testing program. This process took two years and included testing the aircraft in extreme weather conditions.

KEY

△ A380 suppliers

■ Airbus manufacturing sites

Worldwide operation
As well as the 16 main Airbus manufacturing sites in Europe, there are many other suppliers across the world. In addition to those shown above, suppliers are also located in Australia, Japan, Malaysia, and South Korea.

Final destination
The A380's final assembly plant in Toulouse was built especially for the new aircraft. The building is 1,640 ft (500 m) long, 820 ft (250 m) wide, and 151 ft (46 m) high. As well as the main assembly building there is also a separate ground testing hangar.

Inflight testing
The A380 made its maiden flight in April 2005 and received safety certificates from both European and US air authorities in March 2006. Even after this, the A380 still had to undergo 2,500 hours of inflight safety testing. Five aircraft were used for this purpose, with two of them specifically testing things such as aerodynamics, vibration, and the effects of low-speed flying.

Top terminals

Many factors have influenced the growth of air travel, including advances in aviation technology, the expansion of international trade, and the increased affordability of flying. It is now possible to fly to virtually anywhere in the world in under 24 hours. Much of the world's population lives in the northern hemisphere, so most major passenger routes operate in this region.

Air has also become an important method of transporting freight around the world, especially low-weight goods of high value. Many of the main cargo airports are located on principal international trade routes, such as between Asia and the USA.

This map illustrates the top ten busiest passenger and cargo airports in 2005, as well as the largest passenger airports in Africa, Australasia, and Latin America. The takeoff and landings figures include both passenger and cargo flights for each airport.

Anchorage (ANC) USA

Opened: 1953

3rd-busiest cargo airport

Takeoffs and landings (2005): 313,665

Las Vegas (LAS) USA

Opened: 1942

9th-busiest passenger airport

Takeoffs and landings (2005): 605,046

Louisville (SDF) USA

Opened: 1947

10th-busiest cargo airport

Takeoffs and landings (2005): 179,681

Chicago O'Hare (ORD) USA

Opened: 1945

2nd-busiest passenger airport

Takeoffs and landings (2005): 972,248

Los Angeles (LAX) USA

Opened: 1930

5th-busiest passenger and 7th-busiest cargo airport

Takeoffs and landings (2005): 650,629

Atlanta Hartsfield (ATL) USA

Opened: 1946

World's busiest passenger airport

Takeoffs and landings (2005): 980,386

Newark

Dallas/Fort Worth (DFW) USA

Opened: 1974

6th-busiest passenger airport

Takeoffs and landings (2005): 711,878

Longest non-stop scheduled commercial flight –

Memphis (MEM) USA

Opened: 1929

World's busiest cargo airport

Takeoffs and landings (2005): 392,360

Key

Cargo: Total cargo tonnage (in millions of tons) in 2005

3.5+   3.1+   2.3+   1.9+   1.7+   0+

Passengers: Total number of passengers (in millions) in 2005

80+   70+   60+   50+   40+   0+

Mexico City Benito Juárez (MEX) Mexico

Opened: 1950s

Busiest passenger airport in Latin America and the Caribbean

Takeoffs and landings (2005): 332,623

Lying 3 miles (5 km) off the coast of Honshu, Japan, is an artificial island. It was constructed to provide an offshore location for Kansai International Airport. The airport's distance from residential areas means it can operate around the clock. Every day thousands of passengers pass through the long, wing-shaped terminal building.

Kansai International Airport Osaka

Durable building
The terminal building is constructed to withstand earthquakes and typhoon winds.

The passengers

Kansai International is a busy airport—more than 16 million passengers used it in 2005. It means there is a constant flow of people in the terminal, from those waiting to board flights to others who have just disembarked from their aircraft.

Koji
Koji traveled an hour from Kagoshima to take pictures of aircraft. "The Kansai terminal is beautiful."

Hiromi
Hiromi is having a massage while waiting for a flight. "The first time I came to Kansai I thought the architecture was wonderful."

Setsuko
Setsuko is going on vacation with her husband Asani. "We traveled to the airport by train and are catching a plane to Okinawa."

Shirakashi family
"This is our first visit to Kansai International Airport. We came to show our two children the planes taking off and landing."

Gilbert
Gilbert is an engineer from Australia returning after a business trip. "Kansai is very modern and clean."

At the airport
The first floor of Kansai's airport terminal is for international arrivals. Domestic flights are on the second floor, stores and restaurants are found on the third floor, and international departures check-in on the fourth floor.

Terminal trivia

■ Around 45,000 passengers pass through the airport each day.
■ At 1 mile (1.7 km) long, the airport terminal is the largest in the world.
■ The roof is covered with 82,000 steel panels.

■ The arched roof is specially designed to channel fresh air from one side of the terminal to the other.
■ Supporting columns under the terminal can be adjusted if there is any land movement.

■ A bridge connects the airport to the mainland to provide road and rail connections. Travelers can also arrive by high-speed ferry.
■ Passengers are transported through the airport by people-conveyers and elevators.

■ At the top of the airport terminal is the Aeroplaza, a complex containing stores and the island's only hotel.
■ A second runway is planned to enter service in 2007.

London Heathrow (LHR) England

Opened: 1946

3rd-busiest passenger airport

Takeoffs and landings (2005): 477,888

Amsterdam Schiphol (AMS) Netherlands

Opened: 1920

10th-busiest passenger airport

Takeoffs and landings (2005): 420,633

Frankfurt Main (FRA) Germany

Opened: 1936

6th-busiest cargo and 8th-busiest passenger airport

Takeoffs and landings (2005): 490,147

Seoul (ICN) South Korea

Opened: 2001

5th-busiest cargo airport

Takeoffs and landings (2005): 163,575

Tokyo Narita (NRT) Japan

Opened: 1978

4th-busiest cargo airport

Takeoffs and landings (2005): 189,498

Airport codes

There are two types of codes used to identify airports around the world. The first is based on a system set up by the International Air Transport Association (IATA) and is made up of three letters. These codes are used for airline timetables and to identify the origin and destination of passengers' baggage. The second type is a four-lettered International Civil Aviation Organization (ICAO) code. This variety is more comprehensive and includes not only an abbreviation for the airport, but also indicates the region where it is located. The ICAO code is used by air traffic controllers and increasingly by airlines.

Paris Charles de Gaulle (CDG) France

Opened: 1974

7th-busiest passenger airport

Takeoffs and landings (2005): 522,619

Tokyo Haneda (HND) Japan

Opened: 1931

4th-busiest passenger airport

Takeoffs and landings (2005): 295,745

Shanghai (PVG) China

Opened: 1999

8th-busiest cargo airport

Takeoffs and landings (2005): 205,045

Singapore (SIN) Singapore

Opened: 1981

9th-busiest cargo airport

Takeoffs and landings (2005): 208,280

Newark to **Singapore** (18–20 hours)

Air travel

■ About three-quarters of all air traffic operates within and between three regions: Asia, Europe, and North America

■ The world's busiest air route is across the North Atlantic.

■ Flying is more affordable than it ever has been. Developments in technology mean that, in real terms, average air fares are cheaper now than they were in the 1970s.

■ Poland, China, and the Czech Republic are among the countries predicted to experience major growth in international passenger traffic up to 2009.

■ In the same period, China (along with Asia-Pacific countries such as Thailand and Malaysia) is predicted to have the biggest expansion in international freight traffic.

■ Memphis is the world's busiest cargo airport because it is the home of FedEx. UPS has its international headquarters at Louisville, the 10th-busiest air cargo hub.

■ The world's biggest airport in terms of area is Riyadh in Saudia Arabia—it covers approximately 87 sq miles (225 sq km).

Johannesburg (JIA) South Africa

Opened: 1952

Busiest passenger airport in Africa

Takeoffs and landings (2005): 197,335

Hong Kong (HKG) China

Opened: 1998

2nd-busiest cargo airport

Takeoffs and landings (2005): 273,407

Sydney Kingsford Smith (SYD) Australia

Opened: 1920

Busiest passenger airport in Australasia

Takeoffs and landings (2005): 286,827

The workers

From porters to check-in staff, security men to cleaners, the airport employs an army of different workers to ensure that travelers' needs are met. Many jobs operate around the clock, ensuring the smooth running of the airport 24/7.

Eiji and Yukitaka

Pilot Eiji and his copilot Yukitaka work for All Nippon Airways. "We both like to fly Boeing 747s."

Shiori

Flight attendant Shiori works for All Nippon Airways and flies all over Japan. "My favorite route is to Ishigaki Island in the south."

Junzo

Junzo works in the Legend of Concorde restaurant. "The most popular meal is a replica of the food served on board the aircraft."

Kazuko

As one of the airport cleaners, Kazuko works in a team of 30 people. "I enjoy meeting all the foreign people here."

Teruko

Teruko has worked as a radar operator at Kansai for eight years. "The view of the airport in the ocean is something special."

Keizo

Cart operator Keizo started working at the airport soon after it opened in 1995. "This is a very friendly place to work."

Susumu

Maintenance worker Susumu carries out preflight and arrival checks on aircraft during the day. "On the night shift, I do periodic maintenance and general repairs on the aircraft."

People power

- It took 10,000 laborers three years to construct the artificial island upon which the airport is located. The 98-ft (30-m) layer of foundations required rock and soil to be excavated from three mountains.

- Hundreds of staff are needed to work in the airport's 35 restaurants. Most of them serve Japanese food such as sushi and noodles. In addition, there are 26 coffee shops and bars, and 110 stores.

- International flights from Kansai go to 72 cities in 29 different countries.
- Kansai also has connections to 14 domestic cities, including Tokyo Haneda, Sapporo, and Kagoshima.

- Its location means that Kansai is the only airport in Japan allowed to operate at night.
- For visitors wanting to know more about Kansai's history and construction, official guides offer tours of the airport.

Plane spotting

From small, single-seater light aircraft to super-airliners that can carry more than 850 people, the skies are filled with many types of civilian planes. Airports are the best place to spot them, especially the more popular commercial airliners, but most planes flying overhead can be identifed by their wing profile, engine position, and tail shape.

AIRBUS A380-800

The world's largest civilian airliner has two decks and a wing that weighs in at 750 tons. Some versions of the A380 are able to carry up to 853 passengers.

Specifications	
Length	239 ft 6 in (73 m)
Wingspan	261 ft 9 in (79.8 m)
Cruising speed	593 mph (955 km/h)
Passengers	Up to 853

BOEING 747-400

The most successful widebody jet in history, the 747 is continually being upgraded. The 747-400 has raised wing tips for improved aerodynamics, as well as a new flight deck.

Specifications	
Length	231 ft 7 in (70.6 m)
Wingspan	211 ft 4 in (64.4 m)
Cruising speed	567 mph (912 km/h)
Passengers	Up to 524

AIRBUS A340-600

The longest commercial airliner in the world, the A340-600 is used on long-haul routes. As well as transporting passengers, it has a large cargo-carrying capacity.

Specifications	
Length	247 ft (75.30 m)
Wingspan	208 ft 2 in (63.45 m)
Cruising speed	573 mph (923 km/h)
Passengers	Up to 419

ILYUSHIN IL-96M

The Il-96 first flew in the early 1990s and is one of Russia's most advanced airliners. The M is longer than earlier types and can travel nonstop for 6,462 miles (10,400 km).

Specifications	
Length	212 ft 3 in (64.7 m)
Wingspan	197 ft 3 in (60.11 m)
Cruising speed	516 mph (830 km/h)
Passengers	Up to 375

BOEING 767-400

The 767 is often used for crossing the Atlantic Ocean. It has flown this route more times than all other aircraft types combined. The 400 has the longest fuselage in the 767 range.

Specifications	
Length	201 ft 5 in (61.4 m)
Wingspan	170 ft 3 in (51.9 m)
Cruising speed	529 mph (851 km/h)
Passengers	Up to 375

BOEING 737-700

Making its first flight in 1968, the Boeing 737 is in the record books as the most highly produced jet airliner ever. When the range was revamped in 1993, the 737-700 was introduced.

Specifications	
Length	110 ft 3 in (33.6 m)
Wingspan	112 ft 6 in (34.3 m)
Cruising speed	529 mph (851 km/h)
Passengers	Up to 149

AIRBUS A320-200

The first passenger airliner to use computer technology to fly a plane, the A320 set new standards when it was unveiled in 1988. It remains a popular short-range aircraft.

Specifications	
Length	123 ft 3 in (37.57 m)
Wingspan	111 ft 9 in (34.09 m)
Cruising speed	541 mph (870 km/h)
Passengers	Up to 164

GULFSTREAM G400

The G400 is a high-specification business jet that can carry eight passengers in ultimate luxury. It is able to travel as fast as many commercial airliners.

Specifications	
Length	88 ft 3 in (26.9 m)
Wingspan	77 ft 9 in (23.7 m)
Cruising speed	528 mph (850 km/h)
Passengers	Up to 8

CESSNA CARAVAN

One of the world's most successful light aircraft, the Caravan can be used for a variety of purposes including passenger transportation and cargo-carrying.

Specifications	
Length	37 ft 7 in (11.5 m)
Wingspan	52 ft 2 in (15.9 m)
Top speed	212 mph (341 km/h)
Passengers	Up to 14

Air identity

From the early days of commercial passenger flight, airlines realized how important it was to have a strong corporate identity. In a competitive market, it made their brand stand out and could attract potential customers. The most visible place to display a design is across the tailplane, which can be seen from the ground when an aircraft is up in the air. Other methods of promoting airline identity include colorful advertising posters and designer uniforms for the crew.

Air France tail (1950s) United Airlines tail (1930s) SAS tail (1970s)

Lufthansa advertising (1960s) United Airlines advertising (1930s)

Tailplanes
Whether simply displaying the name or livery of an airline or illustrating a more elaborate motif such as the British Airways example above, tailplanes are the most important and prominent identity space on an aircraft.

UFTHANSA

British Airways advertising (2000s)

Deutsche Lufthansa advertising (1930s)

Air France advertising (1950s)

BRITISH AIRWAYS HOLIDAYS

DEUTSCHE LUFT HANSA

o Late
et Away!

The MacMichaels fly to Italy on the world's largest airline

He's William MacMichael of Sherman, Texas, a production manager for the world's largest manufactu of electronic equipment. She's Betty Jane. And the boy in the ten gallon hat is Tommy, their twelve y old son. Why did they choose Air France to Italy? Too many reasons to list here. But to name a f direct jets to Paris from Houston (Air France also has jet flights from New York, Chicago, Los Ange Anchorage, Montreal and Mexico City.) Ideal connections to Italy. (Air France serves more cities in Eur with jets than any other airline.) Fabulous food. (It's French!) Incomparable service. (It's French!) I jet fares. (None lower on any other airline.) Now what's your reason for flying Air France this ye

AIR FRANCE

British Overseas Airways Corporation (BOAC) uniform (1950s)

Air France uniform (2005)

B·O·A·C

United Airlines uniform (1960s)

In-flight fashion
Airlines dress their crew in smart clothes, with flight attendants wearing uniforms in the color of the airline. Some airlines will provide forms of local dress for their crew—female Air India crew, for example, wear saris on flights. Others commission famous designers to create their uniforms. In 2005, Air France asked the world-renowned designer Christian Lacroix to come up with the airline's new uniforms.

Pie in the sky

Physical changes to the human body when flying in a plane mean that a lot of thought has to go into creating airline meals. During a flight, air pressure affects the taste buds so your sense of taste diminishes. In addition, flying at altitude dehydrates the body, so only low levels of salt, which itself dehydrates, can be used. Food is prepared on the ground and then transferred to the aircraft before being reheated in the galleys and served up.

Preparing the food
Every day, hundreds of thousands of meals are prepared for air travelers around the world. Methods to ensure that the food tastes good in the air include slow simmering, which retains more nutrients than if cooked at normal speed, and pressure-cooking, where meals are cooked, vacuum-packed, and then placed into ice-cold water to retain their freshness. Techniques such as deep-frying are avoided because they do not reheat well.

gourmet

213

...ading up

...e kitchens are usually located near airports so that the food ...es not need to travel far to the aircraft. Most in-flight food ...mpanies also incorporate refrigeration facilities where meals ... be kept fresh before being loaded onto the aircraft. Once ...the plane, the food is moved into storage containers situated ...the galley. The airline crew will then reheat the food before ...ving it up to the passengers.

Dining in style

As well as comfortable seats with plenty of legroom, first- and business-class passengers receive top-quality food served on china plates. Even though the preparation techniques are the same as for economy-class food, final presentation touches are often added by the stewards. Passengers can select what they want to eat from a comprehensive menu, which can include duck, veal, or lobster, washed down with complimentary fine wines.

Standard fare

Airlines provide different menus depending on what class ticket a passenger has bought. On long-haul flights, some airlines will offer a choice of two main meals, and there is often a salad and roll included as well. A vegetarian option or other specialist meal can be ordered, but the airline needs to be informed at least 24 hours before the flight. The packaging, plates, and cutlery in economy class are usually made of plastic.

Design for Chunks

In 2001, a design company invited a number of designers to decorate sick bags with their own individual artwork. It was such a success that it turned into an annual event. In 2004, the 20 best sick bags from the fourth Design for Chunks competition were featured on Virgin Atlantic's flights for six months.

Ralph the Robot

YOU 4 MISSING

RELAX.
YOU'LL BE
FEELING FINE
IN NO TIME

pukeⓥpet

DO NOT FILL ABOVE THIS LINE

pukeⓥpet

Sick bags

Air-sickness bags used to be functional objects found inside aircraft seat pockets, but they have now developed into a specialist art form. Some have even become collectors' items, with hundreds of dollars being paid for rare bags in online auctions.

ZOOK!

vouwen — fold — doblar

vouwen — fold — doblar

prullezakje
disposal bag
bolsa para desperdicios

吐袋

for a clean feeling

Cabin collectibles
For collectors, sick bags like this "Dusty the Kangaroo" example made by KLM in 1983 are highly prized. Even more valuable are bags dating from before 1970 and those produced by airlines that are no longer in business, such as Pan Am, Trans World Airlines (TWA), and Sabena.

The science of air sickness

■ Air sickness is a type of motion sickness. It is caused when, during irregular movement, the brain gets confused by mixed signals from sensors (especially in the inner ear and eyes) that indicate the position of the body. It is most likely to occur while an aircraft is going through turbulence.

■ Symptoms of air sickness include nausea, vomiting, sweating, headaches, and a loss of color in the cheeks.

■ Only certain people are susceptible to air sickness, but it is not known why they are more prone than others.

■ Ways of avoiding air sickness before getting on an aircraft include carrying out specific exercises and wearing a wrist band that acts on a pressure point. For those who suffer badly, medication can be prescribed to calm the inner ear and prevent imbalance.

■ Tips for helping prevent air sickness while on a plane include choosing a seat over the wing—the most stable part of the aircraft in flight—and focusing on distant objects rather than close ones. It is better to look out of the window than to read a book or watch a movie.

Lined for strength
Most sick bags come in a standard rectangular shape and are made of paper with a thin plastic or wax interior lining. Swissair produces a bag that can also be used as an envelope to send camera films off to be developed.

AIR CHINA

AEROFLOT

SWISSAIR

AIR INDIA

CATHAY PACIFIC

KOREAN AIR

KLM

CARGO

Air transportation is much quicker than sending goods by sea. Some cargo planes are owned by airlines specializing in freight, while others are part of bigger, passenger-carrying fleets. These planes have transformed people's lives. Thanks to them, nothing is more than 24 hours away. Day and night, planes travel the skies with holds full of urgent mail or perishable goods such as fruit, vegetables, and exotic flowers.

Air freight facts

- ■ FedEx is the world's biggest transportation company. Its cargo airline, FedEx Express, is based in Memphis, Tennessee.

- ■ In 2003, the FedEx "Panda Express" transported two giant pandas from Beijing, China, to Memphis Zoo.

- ■ The American firm UPS (United Parcel Service) delivers more than 15 million packages around the world each day.

- ■ British Airways' Perishable Handling Centre (PHC) deals with more than 80,000 tons of fresh produce every year.

- ■ Perishables make up 11 percent of all air freight in terms of weight.

- ■ About 70 percent of all the perishables that enter the USA arrive at Miami airport.

- ■ NASA's Super Guppy can carry a maximum load of 54,454 lb (24,700 kg).

Loading up

No other aircraft has a fuselage as high as the Airbus Beluga's and none can match its cargo capacity. The plane's "forehead" lifts up to reveal a 49,440-cu ft (1,400-cu m) cargo bay that can carry large aircraft parts and International Space Station components.

Airbus Beluga

Named after the Beluga whale on account of its size and shape, this aircraft was built specifically to transport components for Airbus airliners to assembly plants across Europe. Airbus is jointly owned by French, British, German, and Spanish aerospace companies.

Cargo carrier
Founded in 1971, the FedEx Corporation now flies parcels to more than 220 countries and territories around the world. Its fleet of around 700 aircraft is backed up by 43,000 vans, cars, and motorcycles. The company can transport packages between major cities in a matter of hours. Between 2008 and 2011, FedEx will take delivery of ten Airbus A380 freighters, the world's largest cargo planes.

Super Guppy
The US space agency, NASA, uses an aircraft called the Super Guppy to move International Space Station components and other outsize cargo items. Based on a military Boeing aircraft, the Super Guppy has a hinged nose that opens for easy loading and a 25-ft- (7.6-m-) wide fuselage. The aircraft also has rails and rollers in its cargo bay that can be used to secure and move pallets.

Lower engine
cowling

Rear tire

Wheel

Caliper

Axle

Axle nut

Cotter pin

Axle fixing bolts

Rear wheel fairing (left)

Rear wheel fairing (right)

Spars, ribs, and skins of
left wing assembly

Aileron

Flap

Taking it apart

The majority of parts on the Zodiac XL are made from aluminum alloy. Its light weight and strength makes it an ideal material for aircraft construction. The various sections of the aircraft are joined using "blind" rivets. These only need inserting on one side, which is easier than working with conventional rivets that are inserted on one side and secured on the other. Once the Zodiac has been assembled, it is painted and tested before being given a certificate of airworthiness to officially allow it to fly.

Preformed instrument console

Compass

Altimeter

Airspeed indicator

Radio with GPS unit (top) and encoding transponder (bottom)

Oil temperature gauge

Water temperature gauge

Fuel gauge (left tank)

Fuel gauge (right tank)

Pressure gauge

Voltage meter

Hour meter

Top engine cowling

Switches

Canopy

Engine

Engine mounting

Oil tank

Gascolator

Fuselage

Main spring landing gear

Light aircraft

The Zodiac XL is a kit plane. It can be built with totally separate components or by using a quick-build kit where some sections are preassembled. Many parts have already been cut and riveted, so only basic tools are needed to put the plane together—on average, it takes less than 500 hours to build. And you can then take to the air to enjoy your handywork!

Plane in a box

Apart from the engine and instrument dials, all the Zodiac XL's parts are shipped in a wooden crate. To help buyers build the plane, a manual CD is included, containing instructions, photos, graphs, and technical drawings.

Customizing the plane

Buyers can choose a number of different options, including a range of engines from 100 to 125 horsepower, two- or three-bladed propellers, and a choice of vinyl or leather seats.

Bubble vision

The aircraft's "bubble" canopy gives
the pilot and copilot 360-degree vision.
Not only does this make the journey more
enjoyable, but it provides an added safety
feature because light aircraft pilots often
use landmarks on the ground
to help them navigate.

Comfortable cockpit

At 3.67 ft (1.12 m) wide, the cabin is large for a light
aircraft. The pilot sits in the left-hand seat, but flying
controls on both sides allow the copilot to fly the plane
at any time. Among the aircraft's dials and control
panels are an altimeter (which measures altitude),
a radio to communicate with other pilots,
and a speedometer—the Zodiac XL
cruises at 135 mph (217 km/h).

Fuel tank

Nose rib

Fiberglass
wingtip

Main spar

Red navigation
light (left wing)

Power supply
for strobe lights

Pitot/static air-speed
measurement tubes

Radio antenna

Landing lights

Green navigation
light (right wing)

Power supply for
strobe lights

Nose skin for
rudder

Rib

Fuel tank selector
switch

Spar

Rear rib

Tail light
fitting

Tail light fitting
and bolts

Rear rib

Tail light housing

Tail light and
eyelets

Tail light
lens

Nose wheel fork

Axle and nuts

Nose rib

Rear rib

Axle

Caliper

Wheel

Axle fixing bolts

Axle nut

Rear tire

Nuts, bolts, and attachments

Propeller

Nose gear strut

Wheel and bearings

Front tire

Doubler

Rudder control horn

Rear skin for rudder

Fiberglass stabilizer tip

Front wheel fairing section (right)

Front wheel fairing section (left)

Vertical tail fairing

Elevator

Blind rivets

Fuel line and fittings

Control cable

Seat belt

Seats

Cleco® fastening tool

Cleco® fasteners

Bag of blind rivets

Seat belt

Horizontal stabilizer

Fiberglass stabilizer tip

Managing the skies

In the USA alone, about 75,000 aircraft take off from airports every day, with many thousands more passing through the country's air space. This is why the work of air traffic controllers is vital to keep planes from colliding in midair. Some controllers work in towers at airports to coordinate aircraft taking off and landing, while others are based in regional centers where they monitor aircraft en route to their destinations.

It takes between one and four minutes for an aircraft to land and leave a runway, allowing about 30 landings an hour.

Radar technology was first invented in 1922, but it was not until the 1950s that it had developed enough for use in air traffic control.

Control towers are high so that controllers can get a good view of the runway. The glass in the tower is angled outward to reduce the sun's glare.

At one of the world's busiest airports, Chicago O'Hare, planes take off and land every 40 seconds during peak periods.

Before radio and radar, controllers on the ground would communicate to pilots via light signals and giant information boards.

It can take up to four years to qualify as an air traffic controller. Trainees must be able to make decisions quickly under pressure.

International regulations state that there must be at least 5 miles (8 km) horizontal distance between aircraft in the sky.

There are 20 en-route air traffic control centres in the USA, with up to 150 people on duty during the busiest periods.

Airport control towers monitor air traffic up to about 56 miles (90 km) from the airport and 10,000 ft (3,048 m) above it.

Some noncomputerized en-route control centers still use strips of paper to record aircraft progress.

Stacking occurs when planes circle in the air while waiting for the air traffic control center to give them an available runway.

The safe vertical distance between aircraft in the sky is 1,000 ft (305 m) at low altitude and 2,000 ft (610 m) at higher levels.

In the UK, four main en-route air traffic control centers manage up to 6,000 aircraft per day.

Air traffic controllers are in constant communication with weather forecasters so they can divert aircraft around severe storms.

The display screen that controllers use to intepret what aircraft are flying in the vicinity is known as the radarscope.

Advanced computer software assists controllers in scheduling aircraft for takeoff and landing.

A controller is under the most pressure when delays due to bad weather or technical faults create a backlog of planes.

In the USA, potential candidates for a career as an air traffic controller cannot be older than 30 years of age.

Air traffic controllers must pass a medical exam that tests, among other things, their hearing and vision.

On a long route, a pilot is in contact with a number of air traffic controllers, each of whom oversees their own section of air space.

No matter where a plane is in the world, the air traffic controller and pilot will always communicate in English.

To communicate with control centers, pilots must change radio frequency every time they fly into a new country's air space.

CAA9971
200C 315
BWI ATL
CRJ2 13:32

UAL517
305C↑ 376
CLT DEN
BY33 15:58

CSG3078
060C 262
CLT CMH
J145 14:45

TRS257
330 460
FNT MCO
8712 14:16

RSTS99
370C 308
VGA RDU
8712 13:10

JIA2414
230 462
MEM CLT
CRJ2 13:37

DAL1127
340↑ 384
BUF ATL
B732 13:43

USS5015
340T 256
NYG ORD
BJ1 11:55

MEP409
340↓ 417
MCO MCI
8712 14:57

DAL355
225C↓ 339
CYYZ KATL
BY32 13:10

N204RT
170 334
TYS PDK

AAL1713
300 400
DCA DFW

M7135K
060↑ 190
SPA ATL
BE40 13:17

BAR072
220C↓ 265
CVG SAV
CKJ3 13:41

517A 320
ATL HON
CRJ2 11:59

BWI072
240C↑ 335
SAV GVT
CKJ5 14:05

N9165L
090↓ 190
LAX ATL
BE40 12:47

GFR9019
220T↑ 296
ORD SEA
BT1 13:55

TTY9756
252A 355
CAR GSP
CRJ2 12:32

PPA387
230A 780
ATL WIS
GA72 14:50

XTKS99
570C 508
SAV GVT
A7320 13:34

AHN5078
040A↑ 232
HTW CMH
JU45 12:23

PLG4756
152C 355
DTW GSP
CRJ2 12:32

PAA699
140A↑ 780
ATL ALA
GT72 12:50

CAS510
217D↑ 320
WAS ATL
CRJ2 12:19

Eyes on the skies

All airports that operate regular scheduled flights have an air traffic control tower such as this one in Brussels. The 427-ft (130-m) tower at Kuala Lumpur International Airport, Malaysia, is the world's tallest—its design imitates an Olympic torch.

Space tourism

In one giant leap for tourism, companies are producing commercial spacecraft to take people into space. Since space flights began in the 1960s, only about 500 astronauts have traveled beyond Earth's atmosphere. This figure is set to rocket as new types of craft take off and the cost of space travel drops. Budding astronauts won't need to undergo months of intensive training—several days of preflight simulation and medical screenings will be all it takes to reach the final frontier.

Prized possession

The Ansari X Prize was devised in 1996 to encourage low-cost commercial space travel. The $10 million prize was for the first nongovernment organization to launch a reusable piloted craft into space twice over a period of two weeks. On October 4, 2004, the Tier One Project group won with *SpaceShipOne*.

Blast off!

Around the world, 26 teams took part in the Ansari X Prize competition. Starchaser Industries successfully launched the privately built rocket *Nova* in 2001. However, it was unmanned and reached a height of 1.04 miles (1.68 km), far short of the 62 miles (100 km) necessary to win the prize.

Launch of space tourism

US businessman Dennis Tito was the world's first space tourist. In April 2001, he paid $20 million to board the *Soyuz TM-32* spacecraft. He spent 7 days, 22 hours, and 4 minutes in orbit, and docked at the International Space Station.

In the driving seat

The cockpit of *SpaceShipOne* is surrounded by a protective outer shell to ensure that any problems with the craft will not lead to loss of cabin pressure. The craft has strategically placed windows to give the pilot multiple views of the horizon. These windows have to be small to minimize the weight of the vehicle.

Spaced out

A number of companies provide astronaut training and one even offers zero-gravity flights on an adapted Ilyushin Il-76 aircraft. State-of-the-art technology produces realistic simulation so that passengers can experience weightlessness without actually traveling into space.

The Galactic's adjustable wings adopt a "shuttlecock" shape when reentering Earth's atmosphere so that the craft drifts slowly and gently back down.

Inside the craft, passengers will be able to release their safety straps and float around the cabin to experience weightlessness.

Observation windows will allow passengers to look back at Earth and see more than 1,000 miles (1,610 km) in any direction.

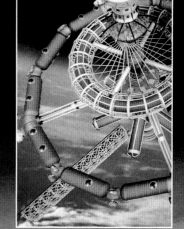

Checking into orbit

Although this hotel is only an artist's impression, vacations in space could become a reality. Space Island Project plans to connect empty space shuttle fuel tanks and create a space hotel.

Beyond the stars

Virgin Galactic, part of British entrepreneur Sir Richard Branson's Virgin Group, is planning space travel for the masses. By offering affordable flights to paying passengers, a trip to space could become as commonplace and hassle-free as boarding an aeroplane. The fleet of spacecraft are based on the Ansari X Prize-winning *SpaceShipOne* design.

Air junk

From broken Boeings to battered B-52 bombers,
all aircraft eventually come to the end of their
useful lives. When planes are no longer able to fly,
they are transported to specialist "graveyard" sites
where they are broken up. In space, there is another type of junk as hundreds
of thousands of pieces that have fallen off rockets and satellites circle the
orbits of Earth and other planets. Although small, these bits of debris pose
a threat to active space missions and need to be constantly monitored.

Salvage and meltdown

Dismantling sites are often located in deserts where the hot, dry conditions preserve the planes and prevent rust. Some working parts can be repaired and then sold on to be used in other aircraft, while the remaining components will be melted down and transformed into objects such as cans for sodas.

Military graveyard

More than 5,000 old fighters and bombers, mainly B-52s, are stored at the Davis Monthan Air Force base in Arizona. Some are scrapped, others are kept for their spare parts, while a few are transformed into "drones." These small planes do not have pilots but are flown by remote control, and onboard cameras are used to take pictures of the ground.

Space junk

There are an estimated one million pieces of artificial debris floating out in space. Many, such as those surrounding this Lunar Module, are created by spacecraft after they separate from the rockets that take them out into space. Even though most space junk is no bigger than a pebble, it is a threat to spacecraft because it is traveling at about 17,398 mph (28,000 km/h).

Testing for debris

A spacecraft called the Long Duration Exposure Facility spent almost six years in space carrying out a number of experiments. One measured the amount of meteorite particles and artificial debris in Earth's orbit. The mission concluded that about 40 percent of the debris in low orbit was artificial, a much higher figure than had been expected.

Record highs

Most aircraft landings in 24 hours
In May 2001, American Thomas Bishop made 442 takeoffs and landings in his light aircraft at an airfield in Texas over a 24-hour period.

Fastest jet
In 1964, the two-seat high-speed US military jet called the Blackbird flew in excess of Mach 3 – three times the speed of sound.

Busiest passenger airport
The world's busiest airport is Atlanta Hartsfield, which dealt with 85,905,000 passengers and had 980,386 takeoffs and landings in 2005.

Longest time spent in a hot-air balloon
In 1999, Englishman Brian Jones and Swiss Bertrand Piccard flew around the world, setting off from Switzerland and landing in Egypt 19 days, 21 hours, and 47 minutes later.

Oldest wing-walker
Born on August 21, 1912 in Zimbabwe, William Green did a wing-walk 88 years, 10 months, and one week later. This record-breaking wing-walk took place in South Africa on 14 July 2001.

Largest passenger aircraft
Launched in 2000 and set to enter service in 2007, the Airbus A380 is 239 ft 6 in (73 m) long and has a wingspan of 261 ft 9 in (79.8 m). It will be able to carry over 850 passengers.

Most aircraft taking off in one hour
On September 10, 2004, Dutchman Meine Brecnlhaar celebrated his wedding anniversary by arranging for 87 aircraft to take off in one hour from Holland's Lelystad Airport.

Most parachute descents
By the end of 2005, American Don Kellner had made more than 36,000 free-fall skydives. His first parachute jump was 44 years earlier.

Highest hot-air balloon altitude
On 6 June 1988, Per Lindstrand flew his Colt 600 hot-air balloon up to a height of 64,997 ft (19,811 m) over Texas.

From packed passenger planes to heavy helicopters, hot-air balloons to paper airplanes, wing-walkers to skydivers, the record books are packed with high-fliers. And with more and more people taking to the skies, either looking for thrills or purely for travel purposes, some of these records may be broken, while others will be created.

Largest model aeroplane collection
From 1936 up until his death in 2003, American John Kalusa had constructed 5,829 wooden airplanes. The collection is housed at the Embry-Riddle Aeronautical University in Arizona.

Most aircraft flown in as a passenger
In 1943, Englishman Edwin A Shackleton went on his first flight in a De Havilland DH 89. By July 2004, he had flown in 806 different types of aircraft, including airships, hot-air balloons, and microlights.

Fastest circumnavigation on scheduled flights
In January 1980, Englishman David J Springbett circumnavigated the globe in 44 hours and 6 minutes. His 23,068-mile (37,124-km) trip started and finished in Los Angeles.

Longest paper airplane flight
American Ken Blackburn hand-launched his paper airplane at the Georgia Dome, Atlanta, in October 1998—it stayed aloft for 27.6 seconds.

Fastest microlight flight around the world
Englishman Colin Bodill qualified as a microlight instructor in 1980. He became a recordbreaker in 2000 after flying around the world in 99 days.

Largest helicopter
The world's largest helicopter is the Russian Mil Mi-26. It is 131 ft (40 m) in length and has a maximum take-off weight of 123,468 lb.

Fastest propeller-driven aircraft
The Soviet Tu-95/142 can travel at a top speed of 575 mph (925 km/h). This incredible speed is achieved by four powerful turboprop engines, each driving huge eight-blade propellers.

Largest airship
This record is shared by two German airships—the Hindenburg (LZ 129) and Graf Zeppelin II (LZ 130). Both airships measured 803 ft (245 m) long.

Most scheduled flights in 24 hours
In 1990, Englishman Michael Bartlett made 42 scheduled flights with Heli Transport, traveling between Cannes, Monaco, Nice, and Sophia Antipolis.

The winglike fin is designed to help the skydiver glide along on air currents.

Flight of fancy

In 2003, Austrian Felix Baumgartner took the sport of skydiving to a futuristic level. With a 6-ft- (1.8-m-) long carbon-fiber fin strapped to his back, he leapt from a plane and rode air currents for 22 miles (35 km), crossing the English Channel.

Driverless cabs

A pilot scheme of a driverless taxi system is underway in Cardiff, Wales. The computer-controlled ULTra pods collect passengers from pickup points and then travel along elevated rail networks to a passenger's chosen destination.

The pod is designed to carry four passengers, with two seats at the front and rear.

Future travel

The world of transportation is constantly evolving, with new designs and prototypes pushing technological boundaries. Coping with congested urban areas, developing solutions to the problem of a depleting fuel supply, and finding ways to visit the previously unexplored parts of our planet are the driving forces behind much of the innovation. In the space of just a few years, a new idea can become a reality and the technology a commonplace feature of our everyday lives.

Made of fiberglass, each cab's payload weighs 1,103 lb (500 kg).

Annual number of air travel passengers: 2 billion

Largest planned cruise ship: Royal Caribbean are building 1,181-ft (360-m) cruise ship that can carry 5,400 passengers

Predicted number of cars in the world by 2035: More than 850 million

The cabs travel along a purpose-built, 5.3-ft- (1.6-m-) wide elevated track.

Ocean flyer

Powered by two propellers, the Deep Flight Aviator is a submersible that literally flies through ocean water. It can dive at speeds of around 328 ft (100 m) per minute, which is faster than any other submersible. Rudders at the back of the craft allow it to rotate sideways, so the pilot can explore the ocean depths.

Propellers drive the craft forwards at speeds up to 9.2 mph (14.8 km/h).

Future theories

- Warships will increasingly use stealth technologies to make them invisible to radar, and jet engines may be used on ships to propel them through the water.

- On land, high oil prices will put the focus on greener fuels and improvements to public transportation. High-speed rail links will be built and more bicycle routes opened.

- Bigger planes carrying more than 500 passengers will dominate long-haul air travel. More fare-paying passengers will also have the opportunity to venture into space.

The battery-powered ULTra cabs travel at an average speed of 24.6 mph (39.6 km/h).

Fare paid by first space tourist: Dennis Tito paid $20 million for his 2001 space flight

Passenger fare on Virgin Galactic's first suborbital flight in 2007: Each space tourist will pay $200,000 for their space journey

Urban transporter

Designed to be used in pedestrian areas, the Segway HT is a two-wheeled transportation device. Electrically powered, the rider stands on a platform and controls the self-balancing Segway using the handles. A nifty device for getting around urban areas, it has been tested in the USA by police on patrol.

A flat tire can cause the car to express sadness by glowing blue.

Mood car

Japanese company Toyota has developed a car that shows feelings. The driver's voice, pulse, and perspiration levels are monitored to gauge emotions and the front of the POD car lights up in different colors to indicate mood. If the car glows red for anger, soothing music is played to the driver.

On the GO!

It has been quite a journey making this book. In fact, the total distance the team traveled was 116, 545 miles (187,561 km), which is almost five times the circumference of the Earth! We sent photographers to many different countries to take pictures of boats, car towers, airports, stunt riders, kit planes, and much more. We clocked up thousands more miles commuting to and from work every day. The book's journey continued after our work was finished. Packed into a container ship, it traveled from Hong Kong to reach bookshops and other outlets all over the world.

Tracks and tires

We clocked up nearly 2,000 bus trips, more than 3,000 train journeys, 24 flights, 120 car rides, 60 motorbike rides, and 10 ferry trips—not to mention a considerable distance by foot.

✈ 24 🚴 60 🚆 3000 🚌 2000 🚤 10 🚗 120 🚢 1

Mexico, Missouri
After photographing every part of a Zodiac XL plane, the team got to fly in one.

Savannah, Georgia
The ease with which these Gulfstream planes were put together was recorded.

New York City
We spent three days at Grand Central Terminal talking to staff and commuters.

Dakar, Africa
As the Dakar Rally drivers raced across Africa, we followed their route.

Exeter, UK
Motorcross rider Jason Smyth dazzled us with spectacular stunts.

Southampton, UK
We watched a racing sailboat being assembled and photographed its parts.

London, UK
Staff and commuters on the London Underground network gave us their views.

187561 kilometers   116545 miles

PASSENGER TICKET AND BAGGAGE CHECK
SUBJECT TO CONDITIONS OF CONTRACT

HELLAS JET

2161144958

FLIGHT COUPON 2 OF 2

O ÄTHENS   T4 304   E 14AUG 1740OK14AUGT4AUG
LONDON HEATHROW
NONREF/VALID ON T4 ONLY

GBP   119.00
GB   5.00
UB   10.40
XT   21.70
GBP   156.

2 681 2161144958 0

Hannover, Germany
The incredible Car Towers
we visited are part of
a motoring theme park.

9 Dresden, Germany
We photographed the
assembly line at Volkswagen's
Gläserne Manufacktur.

10 Bologna, Italy
Ducati let us reduce one of
their racing motorbikes into
its component parts.

11 Delhi, India
Traveling on buses all over
Delhi gave us a unique view
of the city.

12 Sydney, Australia
For the photoshoot on the
Sydney ferries, having good
sea legs was an advantage.

13 Osaka, Japan
The sleek architecture is
why we chose a feature on
Osaka Airport.

14 Hong Kong, China
The printed books were
packed into containers and
shipped from Hong Kong.

Index

Index

Acknowledgments

DK would like to thank:

Idris Ahmed, Andy Crawford, Jim Green, Barry Hayden, Dave King, David Mager, Kenny McLeish, and Chris Stowers for photography; Darren Robert Awauh and Mark Longworth for illustrations.

Niki Foreman, Hoa Luc, and Kate Scarborough for editorial assistance; Joe Conneally and Jim Green for design assistance; Indexing Specialists (UK) Ltd, Hove, for the index.

Mark Ledington from the Morgan Motor Company; Bartosz Piechota and Craig Outhwaite from Evans Cycles, Waterloo Road, London; Ludovica Benedetti, Massimo Davoli, and Livio Lodi at Ducati, Bologna; Sebastien Heintz, Roger Dubbert, Hick Heintz, and all the staff at Zenith Aircraft Company; Alex Southon, Rob Britton, Jim Hood, and RS Racing for the use of an RS700. For further details on the RS range visit www.rssailing. com; Jason Smyth, motocross stuntman. See www.adrenaline tour.com; Nichola Batten at the Volkswagen Autostadt, Wolfsburg; Alexander Skibbe at the Gläserne Manufaktur, Dresden; GoinGreen for use of Reva G-Wiz. For more information see www.goingreen.co.uk; Daniel M Brucker at Grand Central Terminal; Valerie Buckingham and Taiyaba Khatoon for help organizing the Delhi photoshoot; Laura Wallace and the Emergency Response Unit team at Vauxhall, London; Belinda Luton and Ann Laker from the London Underground Press Office and Shirley Cody from the Film Liaison Office; Daisuke Komine from Kansai International Airport Co., Ltd; Tomoko Matusi from All Nippon Airways Co., Ltd; Kenji Makino from Kansai International Airport Office, Osaka Regional Civil Aviation Bureau, Ministry Of Land, Infrastructure, and Transport; Keiko Yokoh, Nicolas Dhuez, and Yumiko Tahata for help with the Kansai Airport photoshoot; Carol Wiley for interviewing passengers and staff of Sydney Ferries; the team at Sydney Ferries; Robert Baugniet, Julie McCoy, and all the staff at Gulfstream; Steve McMahon from Aerosite.net; Mark Jackson from Slam City Skates, London; Selina Da Silva from the 100 Marathon Club; Maria Aurora Hinayon from Airports Council International; Marcus Hutchinson from America's Cup; Debbi Gibbs and Steve Bailey from Gibbs Aquada; Michael Gallagher at Cunard for QM2 queries.

The publisher would like to thank the following for their kind permission to reproduce their photographs:

(Key: a-above; b-below/bottom; c-center; l-left; r-right; t-top)

1 SuperStock: age fotostock/Javier Larrea. 3 SuperStock: age fotostock/ Brian Bielmann. 4 SuperStock: age fotostock/Liane Cary. 6-7 SuperStock: age fotostock/G.V.P. 8-9 Bluegreen Pictures. 10 The Art Archive: Dagli Orti (1/b). Bridgeman Art Library: Royal Thames Yacht Club, London, UK (5/b). © The Trustees of the British Museum: Chas Howson (2/b); Ivor Kerslake (2/t). DK Images: Judith Miller/Sloans & Kenyon (4/b); courtesy of the National Maritime Museum, London/James Stevenson & Tina Chambers (3/t) (3/b). Exeter Maritime Museum, the National Maritime Museum London: (1/t). © National Maritime Museum, London: James Stevenson (5/t). 10-11 Corbis: Rick Doyle (background). 11 Corbis: Bettmann (2/t) (3/b); MacDuff Everton (5/t); Reuters/Henny Ray Abrams (5/b). 12 Alamy Images: Sami Sarkis (tr). Corbis: Peter Guttman (br). Eye Ubiquitous: Marcus Wilson-Smith (l). World Pictures: (c). 12-13 Alamy Images: Blackout Concepts/Mark Owen (background). 13 Camera Press: Gamma/Bertrand Rieger (bl). Corbis: Sygma/ Christophe Delattre (br). Panos Pictures: Mark Henley (l). SuperStock: age fotostock/Doug Scott (tr). Courtesy of US Navy: JO1 Joseph Krypel (c). 14 Alamy Images: Andy Hallam (tc). Getty Images: The Image Bank/ Sakis Papadopoulos (l). Courtesy of US Navy: PH2 (AW) Jonathan R. Kulp (tr). 14-15 Kos Picture Source: Kris. 15 Bluegreen Pictures: Christian Février (r). 16-17 courtesy Hapag-Lloyd. 18 Alamy Images: Roger Bamber. 19 Alamy Images: Jiri Rezac (br). Getty Images: National Geographic/ Randy Olson (tl); Taxi (tc). Hyundai Heavy Industries: (bl). Reuters: Lee Jae-Won (tr). Courtesy of US Navy: (bc). 20 Alamy Images: G.P. Bowater (l); nagelestock.com (r). Getty Images: Yngve Rakke (cb). Fred Olsen Production AS: (ca). 20-21 Corbis: Gary Braasch (background). 21 Alamy Images: Kos Picture Source (cb). Corbis: Denis Balibouse (tr). Getty Images: Stone/David Frazier (c). SuperStock: John Warden (bl). 22 The Art Archive: Culver Pictures (bc). Getty Images: Gamma/Gilles Mermet. Corbis: Dave G. Houser (br). Getty Images: Hulton Archive (bc/right). Reuters: Eliana Aponte (bc/left). 23 Corbis: (br). Reuters: (l). SuperStock: Hubertus Kanus (r). 24 Getty Images: The Image Bank/Richard A. Brooks (l). Still Pictures: Ron Giling (r). 25 Alamy Images: LeighSmith Images (c). DK Images: Gerald Lopez (r). Still Pictures: Ron Giling (l).

27 Corbis: Dennis Degnan. 32-33 Bluegreen Pictures: Rick Tomlinson. 33 Harvie Allison, www.harvpix.com: (b). Rex Features: Verity Reily Collins (c). courtesy, U.S. Coastguard: PA2 Andy Devilbiss (t). 34 Alamy Images: Dan Burton (tr); Buzz Pictures (6); Stephen Frink Collection (2). Corbis: Eye Ubiquitous/David Cumming (1); Karen Kasmauski (3). Crescent Hydropolis Resorts PLC: (4). Photolibrary: Mark Webster (5). 34-35 Oceanwide Images. 35 Corbis: Bettmann (10); Yogi, Inc. (8). FLPA: Minden Pictures/Norbert Wu (tc). NOAA: (9). Photolibrary: Gerard Soury (cb). Science Photo Library: Alexis Rosenfeld (7). 36-37 Reuters. 37 Empics Ltd. : AP/Bob Child (tr) (b). Courtesy of US Navy: Chief Photographer's Mate John E. Gay (cr). 38 Courtesy of US Navy: PH1 Brien Aho (l). USS George Washington and the U.S. Navy / Gary Ombler: (r/all). 39 USS George Washington and the U.S. Navy / Gary Ombler. 41 SuperStock: Jorge Alvarez (l). 48 Reuters: Paul Pelissier. 49 Corbis: Sygma/Guillaume Plisson (b); Onne van der Wal (t). 50-51 Kos Picture Source: AGM/SEA&SEE/Carlo Borlenghi. 51 Empics Ltd. : DPA (br). 52 Guido Grugnola: (tr). Gilles Martin-Raget: (tl). 52-53 Gilles Martin-Raget. 53 Guido Grugnola: (t). Gilles Martin-Raget: (tc) (tr). courtesy, 118 WallyPower: (cr) (br). 54 Corbis: David Lees (bl). Mary Evans Picture Library: (tr) (cr) (br). courtesy, NYK Cruises: (b). 54-55 Mary Evans Picture Library: (background). 55 The Advertising Archives: (cla) (clb). The Art Archive: Chris Deakes/Private Collection (cl). Empics Ltd. : DPA (r). Fiona Hanson (t). Getty Images: The Image Bank/Larry Gatz (crb). P&O Cruises: (r 1/centre) (bl). Photolibrary: foodpix (cra). 56-57 Corbis: zefa/ Pete Leonard (background). courtesy, Cunard Line. 58-59 All photos courtesy of Gibbs Technologies. 60 Corbis: Rick Doyle. 61 Action Plus: Tom Hauck (l); Philippe Millereau (bl). Alamy Images: Jon Arnold Images/James Montgomery (c). Corbis: Steve Wilkings (t). Getty Images: The Image Bank/Ryan McVay (tr); Stone/Brian Bailey (br). Getty Images: Travelshots.com (l). Imagestate: Hoa-Qui/Jeremy Horner (r). 63 Alamy Images: Carole Hewer (b). SuperStock: age fotostock/Javier Larrea (t). World Pictures: (cb); Anthony Cassidy (ca). 64 Alamy Images: Norma Joseph (tr). Aspasia Coumisis: (cla) (clb). 64-65 Alamy Images: David Kilpatrick. 65 Camera Press: Gamma/Raphael Gaillarde (t). DK Images: Rough Guides/Victor Borg (br). Photos: Klaus Frahm; Design/con Gerkan, Marg und Partner, Architects: (c). Graeme Peacock, www.graeme-peacock.com: (bl). 66-67 Alamy Images: David Robertsson. 68-69 SuperStock: age fotostock/Angelo Cavalli. 70 Corbis: Alex Steedman (3/t). DK Images: Courtesy of the Motorcycle Heritage Museum, Westerville, Ohio (4/b); Courtesy of the National Motor Museum, Beaulieu (5/b); Courtesy of The Science Museum, London (1/t); Courtesy of The Science Museum, London/Clive Streeter (1/b); Courtesy of The Science Museum, London/Mike Dunning (2/b). Science & Society Picture Library: (5/t). 70-71 Corbis: ChromoSohm Inc./Joseph Sohm (background). 71 Action Plus: Richard Francis (4/t). Alamy Images: Motoring Picture Library (5/t). Corbis: Paul Almasy (3/b); Reuters/John Hillery (5/b). DK Images: (c) Imperial War Museum, London/Andy Crawford (1/b); Courtesy of the National Motor Museum, Beaulieu (2/t); Courtesy of Slam City Skates (3/t). Robert Harding Picture Library: Nigel Francis (4/b). Science & Society Picture Library: (1/t). 73 Empics Ltd. : PA/Niall Carson (tr). 80-81 Masterfile: Peter Griffith. 86 Alamy Images: Motoring Picture Library (tr). Corbis: (cr). Getty Images: Hulton Archive/ David Savill (c). TopFoto.co.uk: HIP (l). 86-87 Rex Features: Charles M. Ommanney (c). 87 Reuters: (t). 88 DK Images: National Motor Museum (ca/Mercedes 300SL). 96 courtesy of Reva Electric Car Company Pvt Ltd. , www.goingreen.co.uk. 97 Corbis: Reuters/John Hillery (tr). Getty Images: AFP/Kazuhiro Nogi (cr) (br). courtesy of Reva Electric Car Company Pvt Ltd. , www.goingreen.co.uk: (tl) (bl) (c). 98 Alamy Images: PCL (br). Volkswagen: (tl). 99 Courtesy of Autostadt GmbH, Wolfsburg, Germany: (bl). Roger Gorringe: (bc/right). The Kobal Collection: Walt Disney Pictures/Richard Cartwright (bc/left). Volkswagen: (br). 100 Art Directors & TRIP: Warren Jacobs (l). 101 Alamy Images: David Wall (c). Camera Press: Gamma/Gilles Bassignac (r). Getty Images: National Geographic/Raymond K. Gehman (t); Panoramic Images (cla); Stone/ Robert Van Der Hilst (b). Panos Pictures: Dermot Tatlow (cb). 102 Alamy Images: Gari Wyn Williams (br). Corbis: Benjamin Rondel (l). Getty Images: Taxi/Michael Hart (bc). 103 Alamy Images: Anthony Brown (r); Iain Masterton (tl); Photo Japan (cr); Gari Wyn Williams (clb) (br). Art Directors & TRIP: Keith Cardwell (tc). Getty Images: The Image Bank/Grant Faint (cl). 104 Alamy Images: Pat Behnke (bl). Getty Images: Stone/Will & Deni McIntyre (tl). Paul Vlaar, paul@neep.net: (r). 105 Action Plus: Andy Day (l). Alamy Images: George Blonsky (tr). Getty Images: The Image Bank/John William Banagan (br).

112 Alamy Images: Chris P. Batson (tl); David Gordon (b/Glasgow); Megapress (b/Mexico City); Natalie Pecht (b/Buenos Aires); Robert Harding Picture Library Ltd. /Sylvain Grandadam (b/Berlin). Camera Press: Scanpix/Tone Georgsen (b/Oslo). Masterfile: Steve Craft (b/ Toronto). Rex Features: Andrew Drysdale (b/Budapest); Sipa Press (tr). 113 Alamy Images: Iain Masterton (tl); Robert Harding Picture Library Ltd. /Sylvain Grandadam (b/St Petersburg); Neil Setchfield (b/Singapore); TNT Magazine (tc); Visual & Written SL/Kike Calvo (b/Hong Kong); Colin Walton (b/Melbourne). Corbis: Reuters/Lee Jae-Won (b/ Pyongyang); David Sailors (b/Cairo). Panos Pictures: Paul Smith (b/ Kolkata). Rex Features: JD/Keystone USA (tr). 114 Alamy Images: AW Photography (t/Hong Kong); Pat Behnke (c/Brussels); Robert Fried (b/ Madrid); Cris Haigh (c/Bangkok); Nic Hamilton (t/Prague); Jon Hicks (t/ Singapore); Iain Masterton (t/Moscow) (b/Osaka); Beren Patterson (b/ Buenos Aires); Marco Regalia (c/Lisbon); Neil Setchfield (c/Tokyo); Jack Sullivan (c/Vienna); Peter Titmuss (t/Rotterdam). Camera Press: Scanpix/ Jens Noergaard Larsen (t/Copenhagen); TSPL/Robert Perry (t/Rome); Corbis: B.S.P.I. (b/Stockholm); David Sailors (b/Los Angeles). Masterfile: Bryan Reinhart (b/Salzburg). 115 Alamy Images: StockAbcd (br). Art Directors & TRIP: (tl). Camera Press: Gamma/S009 (t/Pyongyang); Gamma/Yannis Kontos (t/Athens); laif/Krause (ca/Cairo); Gamma/Eric Vandeville (t/Naples). Construction Photography.com: Xavier de Canto (t/ Barcelona). Corbis: Alex Steedman (t/London). Getty Images: National Geographic/Richard Nowitz (bl); The Image Bank/Harald Sund (t/St Petersburg). Lonely Planet Images: Bradley Mayhew (ca/London). Rex Features: Henryk T. Kaiser (ca/Warsaw). Still Pictures: Ron Giling (ca/ Mexico City). SuperStock: age fotostock/Gonzalo Pérez Mata (cb/ Valencia); age fotostock/Bartomeu Amengual (cb/Berlin); age fotostock/ Bruce Bi (ca/Beijing); age fotostock/Vin Catania (cb/Paris); age fotostock/ Rudy Sulgan (cb/New York); age fotostock/Renaud Visage (cb/ Barcelona). 116 NASA. 117 Science Photo Library: John Reader. 118 Alamy Images: Worldwide Picture Library/John Cleare. 119 Alamy Images: StockShot/Dave Willis (t). Corbis: Reuters/Andrew Wong (br). Impact Photos: Mark Cator (bl). 120 Lonely Planet Images: Margie Politzer (l). Chris Stowers: (r). 121 Action Plus: Steve Bardens (bc); Richard Francis (cr). Alamy Images: www.gerardbrown.co.uk (cl). Corbis: Larry Kasperek (r); Chris Lisle (br); Don Mason (tr). Empics Ltd. : AP/Tina Fineberg (tl). AP (c). Getty Images: AFP/Javier Soriano (bl); Stone/Paul Chesley (c). 128 Action Plus: Franck Faugere (r). Empics Ltd : AP/ Christophe Ena (l). 129 Corbis: Tim de Waele (tr). Empics Ltd. : DPA/ Bernard Papon (tc); AP/Alessandro Trovati (l). 130 Corbis: Jon Hicks (r). Still Pictures: Jean-Léo Dugast (c). 131 Camera Press: Gamma (bl). Empics Ltd. : AP/Koji Sasahara (tc); PA/Stefan Rousseau (r). 132 Action Plus: Glyn Kirk. Action Images: Reuters/Seth Wenig (r). 133 Action Images: Reuters/Mike Segar (r). 134 Alamy Images: Joe Tree (c). Kenny McLeish: (tc/ left) (b). 135 Alamy Images: Buzz Pictures (tl). Camera Press: Gamma/Neema Frederic (tc/right). Masterfile: Brad Wrobleski (r). Kenny McLeish: (tc/ left) (b). 136 Alamy Images: Chris Fredriksson (tc). Bryan and Cherry Alexander Photography: (bl). Camera Press: laif/Heuer (cr). Corbis: Florio (br). Empics Ltd. : PA/Andrew Parsons (cl). Phil Orsman: (tr). 137 Corbis: Anders Ryman. 138 Adams Picture Library: Alan Moore (clb). Alamy Images: Roberto Aquilano (bl); Ian Leonard (br). Rex Features: Shout (crb). 138-139 Corbis: Patrick Bennett. 140 Alamy Images: Trevor Smithers ARPS (cra). Corbis: epa/R.B. Bangash (crb); Lester Lefkowitz (tr); Anthony Njuguna (bl); Richard T. Nowitz (cra). Masterfile: Allan Davey (tl). Corbis: age fotostock/Andre Maslennikov (cr). 141 Getty Images: The Image Bank/ Thomas Schmitt. 142 Alamy Images: Kim Karpeles (r). Corbis: John H. Clark (l). 143 Robert Haught, AllMoniseter.com: (c) (b). 144 Corbis: Gary Kuther. 145 Alamy Images: guichaoua (bl). Corbis: Jim Zuckerman (br). Robert Harding Picture Library: Premium Stock (r). SuperStock: age fotostock/Michael S. Nolan (tl). 146 Action Plus: Eric Vargiolu (ca). Getty Images: AFP/Martin Bureau (r). Mitsubishi Motor Sports: (b). Daniel Roeseler: (l). 146-147 Mitsubishi Motor Sports: (t/legs 1 to 16). 147 Daniel Roeseler: (br). 148 Getty Images: China Photos. 149 Getty Images: AFP/Peter Parks (t); China Photos (r) (c). 150 Alamy Images: isifa Image Service s.r.o. (tr). Orient-Express Hotels Trains & Cruises: (tl). 150-151 Corbis: Carl & Ann Purcell. 151 The Blue Train: (bc). Camera Press: laif/Heuer (tr). Corbis: Jeremy Horner (tc/ right); Sygma/Richard Smith (br). Orient-Express Hotels Trains & Cruises: (tc/left). Rex Features: (b). 152-153 Getty Images: The Image Bank/Tomek Sikora (background). 154 Corbis: Lucidio Studio Inc.. (br). 160 Action Plus: Icon SMI/Brian Cleary (l). Getty Images: Clive Mason (r). 161 Alamy Images: Tony Watson (b). Empics Ltd. : AP/Al Behrman

(tr). Getty Images: AFP/Valery Hache (ca). Courtesy of McLaren Cars Limited, www.mclarencars.com: — (tl). Keith Scott/rallyxpics.com: (br). 165 Corbis: Ted Soqui (b). 166 Corbis: Sygma/David Brauchli (r). Garry Stuart: (bl) (bc). 167 Alamy Images: Rod Lorance (tl). Getty Images: AFP/ Marcus Brandt (tc). 168 Action Images: Lee Mills (br). Alan Whale. 169 Action Plus: Richard Francis (tr). Action Images: Sporting Pictures/ Simon Miles (br); Neil Tingle (b). Alan Whale: (l). 178-179 Corbis: zefa/ Klaus Hackenberg. 180 Corbis: (4/b) (5/t); Leonard de Selva (3/b). DK Images: Courtesy of The Science Museum, London/James Stevenson (4/ t). Getty Images: Hulton Archive (3/b). Science Museum, London: (1/b). 181 Aviation Picture Library: (2/t). aviation-images.com: (5/b). Camera Press: (3/t). Corbis: Bettmann (4/t). Empics Ltd. : AP/Fabrice Coffrini (5/t). NASA: (3/b) (4/b); Dryden Flight Research Center (1/b). Science Photo Library: Novosti (2/b). TRH Pictures: (1/t). 182 SuperStock: Steve Vidler. 183 SuperStock: Witold Skrypczak. 184 21st Century Airships Inc.: (r). Rex Features: Lehtikuva Oy (br). courtesy of ZLT, Zeppelin Luftschifftechnik: (bl) (tl). 185 courtesy of ZLT, Zeppelin Luftschifftechnik. 186 Getty Images: Jump Run Productions (c); Stone/Dan Smith (b). 186-187 Getty Images: Jump Run Productions. 187 Imagestate: Andy Belcher (br); Tom Sanders (cb) (tr). Rex Features: Simon Ward (ca). 188 aviation-images.com: Mark Wagner (t). Empics Ltd. : AP/Rob Swanson (b). 189 AirTeamImages.com: Gary Watt (br). aviation.images. com: Mark Wagner (tr). courtesy Carter Aviation Technologies: Jason Bynum (t). 191 courtesy Gulfstream Aerospace Corporation: (t) (br). 192 aviation-images.com: Mark Wagner (t). 192-193 Alamy Images: Mark Hamilton. 193 Courtesy of U.S. Air Force: (r). 194-195 Denis Gliksman, http://www.la-grange-numerique.com. 198 Airbus: (t) (r). Airbus-image exm company: P. Masclet (bl). aviation-images.com: (cl). 199 Airbus: (r). Airbus-image exm company: H. Gousse (br). 208 SuperStock: Pixoi Ltd. (bl/background) (t/background). 209 SuperStock: Pixoi Ltd. (background). 210 Aviation Picture Library: (bc). Corbis: George Hall (c). Jim Green: (l). courtesy, SAS Group: (tc). 210-211 The Advertising Archives: (t) (c) (b). 211 The Advertising Archives: (tl) (cl) (clb) (cr). courtesy Air France: (tr) (crb). Corbis: Dean Conger (r). 212 Photo by Gate Gourmet: (tr). Getty Images: AFP/Yoshikazu Tsuno (br) (tr) (bl). 213 aviation-images.com: Mark Wagner (b). The Flight Collection: Hoare (tc). Slick Shoots (br). Photo by Gate Gourmet: (tr) (tr) (bl). 214 Oksana Badrak, Superhappybunny, www.superhappybunny.com: (5/c). David Blaidock, www.ekaada.com.au: (3/t). Jon Burgerman, www.jonburgerman.com: (4/t). (C) Furi Furi Company: (3/c). Louise Helliwell, www.louisehelliwell. com: (4/c). Syl Hillier, www.tapetentiere.de: (1/c). Patrick Padeau, www. charade-design.com: (2/c). Frederick Sanchez, FFred, www.ffred.net: (6/c). Mark Suppelsa, seventy7.ca: (1/t). Morgan Thomas, www.bwoup. com: (2/t). http://www.vonster.com: (5/c). 215 Airsicknessbags.com: (all). 216 Reproduced with kind permission of Airbus UK: L. Baynes (b). Rex Features: David Hodges (t). 217 AirTeamImages.com: Belpix (t). Camera Press: Gamma/De Malglaive (bl). NASA: Dryden Flight Research Center Tony Landis (bc). 225 Camera Press: Gamma/Photo News/Tanguy Jockmans (r). 226 Corbis: Reuters/Sergei Karpukhin (l). Getty Images: Scaled Composites (r). Starchaser Industries Limited, www.starchaser. co.uk: (c). 226-227 Getty Images: The Image Bank/Kevin Kelley (background). 227 aviation-images.com: Mark Wagner. 228 AP/HO/The Space Island Group (tr). Space Adventures, Ltd. : (bl). courtesy Virgin Galactic: (br). 228 aviation-images.com: Mark Wagner. 229 aviation-images.com: Mark Wagner (t). NASA: (c) (b). 230-231 Getty Images: The Image Bank/Color Day Production. 232 Rex Features: Sipa Press (t). Jay Wade: (br). 232-233 Courtesy of Advanced Transport Systems Ltd. 233 Alamy Images: Joseph Szyszewski (br). Rex Features: (tc) Sipa Press (bl). 234 Getty Images: AFP/Damien Meyer (4/b). 235 Alamy Images: sdbphoto.com (14/b). Courtesy of Ducati: (10/b). 236-237 SuperStock: age fotostock/Frank Lukasseck (c). 238-239 SuperStock: age fotostock/ Frank Lukasseck (r). 240 Getty Images: Stone/Glen Allison (t)

Jacket images: Front: Getty Images: Stone cb; Masterfile: Forest Johnson bc; NASA: NASA Langley Research Center (NASA-LaRC) tc. Spine: Getty Images: Brand X Pictures; Front Endpapers: Corbis: Kim Sayer; Getty Images: The Image Bank/Pete Turner; Back Endpapers: Getty Images: The Image Bank/Pete Turner.

All other images © Dorling Kindersley
For further information see: www.dkimages.com

Textbook of Palliative